42 Rules for Growing Enterprise Revenue

By Lilia Shirman
Foreword by Jill Konrath

E-mail: info@superstarpress.com
20660 Stevens Creek Blvd., Suite 210
Cupertino, CA 95014

First Printing: December 2009
Paperback ISBN: 978-1-60773-000-2 (1-60773-000-6)
Place of Publication: Silicon Valley, California, USA
Library of Congress Number: 2009938516

eBook ISBN: 978-1-60773-001-9 (1-60773-001-4)

Trademarks

Warning and Disclaimer

Praise For This Book!

"The core of growing any venture is deep customer insight. Lilia Shirman gives simple, powerful frameworks, practical action plans, and real-world examples for putting such insight to work. This book should be assigned reading in every business and entrepreneurship course."
Tom Kosnik, Fenwick and West Consulting Professor, Stanford Technology Ventures Program, Stanford University

"Simplistic value claims won't cut it in enterprise accounts. Don't leave sales teams to do the hard work of proving worth on their own. Shirman inspires us to stop "crafting" messages and instead to collaborate with customers to understand how and why we really matter. And then to throw the entire organization behind mattering more."
Rick Jackson, CMO, VMware

"The objective for enterprise solution vendors is to make big deals more repeatable and big accounts more loyal. This is an astute and practical guide to greater customer engagement, more valuable offerings, and go-to-market approaches that produce consistently bigger wins. Keep this useful tool on your desk."
Eugene Lee, CEO, Socialtext

"Shirman presents incisive ideas about understanding markets, quantifying value, and constructing solutions and industry offerings that really matter in the customer's universe. Some of these rules are common sense, but certainly not common practice. Many are completely new takes on demonstrating and delivering value. All are thought provoking and critical reading for every one on your management team."
Gail Ennis, CMO, Omniture

iv

Dedication

To my Mother and my Grandfather Shura, who had the courage to rescue me from a world of repression and hypocrisy, and the foresight to teach me that in any world, it's the human relationships that matter most.

With my everlasting gratitude to my husband Leon for his belief, encouragement, and for demonstrating what writing could be in quality, clarity, and speed.

To Nina and Ally, for their contagious enthusiasm and curiosity, and the ultimate writing inspiration contained in the words, "My mom is an author!"

Acknowledgments

Nothing helps communicate an idea better than a real-life example. The stories of how the rules look in practice came from dozens of business leaders who generously shared their experiences and insights. My deepest gratitude goes out to these generous and wise souls. They include Charlie Born, Michael Browning, Mark Carges, Chris Cook, Jeremy Cooper, Erik Frieberg, Jeff Greenwald, Andrea Holko, Rick Jackson, Judy Ko, Bud Landrum, Eugene Lee, Holly Lugassy, Suzanne McLarnon, David Miner, Dave Munn, Michael Pierantozzi, Pavey Purewal, Rick Schmaltz, Dave Stein, Mark Templeton, and Matt Thompson, along with the scores of colleagues and clients who demonstrate the efficacy of customer relevance and business innovation in their daily work. Thanks also to the creative and talented Monica Girel for turning my rough sketches into visually clear diagrams.

This book is better than I could have ever made it alone thanks to the feedback and encouragement of other authors and business sages. They include Ken Goldberg, Jill Konrath, Tom Kosnik, Phillip Lay, Pam Fox Rollin, and Mari Anne Vanella.

Much credit for this book belongs with my executive editor, but more importantly friend and supporter, Laura Lowell, for her encouragement, guidance, patience, and for setting the definitive example of turning vision into reality.

Contents

Contents

Figures

Foreword by Jill Konrath

Selling to large enterprises is complicated. Selling complex products and solutions to these same organizations is even more difficult.

As I travel around, presenting at sales meetings, professional conferences, and industry events, sales professionals are very open with me about the challenges they face. It's tough to set up meetings with busy decision makers, get them to move off the status quo, and set themselves apart from competitors.

It's not any easier for executives. They're struggling to adapt their companies to the turbulent business environment, stay unique, maintain market share, and drive ongoing growth.

Sound familiar? You probably live with these issues every single day. And everything keeps changing. The large enterprises you sell to are in constant flux. They regularly reorganize, open and close offices or entire divisions, and change emphasis among geographies, products, and brands. The roles, priorities, and identities of decision makers shift. Meanwhile your competitors nip at your heels, as they close in on your once-differentiated offering.

Your own company is also evolving, creating its own new set of challenges. You're introducing new products, implementing new marketing strategies, and launching lead generation initiatives and sales programs. The sheer amount of new information overwhelms a seller's ability to keep up, plus creates internal conflict for their mind share.

In response, they resist or ignore new approaches, and stick to selling what they've sold before, to customers who have bought before, using techniques they used last time. To compound the challenges to field adoption, companies are slashing sales enablement budget. They're keeping reps in the field and out of training.

This prevents the transfer of knowledge required for in-depth business domain expertise. We're left with sales forces that know the product details and the high-level messages, but not the context in which it all comes together. For decision makers, this leads to messaging overload. Every vendor seems to promise a similar set of benefits, but few truly understand the relevance to their organization.

As a result, decision makers mistrust salespeople, tune out their claims and put up barriers to keep them at bay. They have no desire to waste their precious time with product-pushing peddlers who are under extreme pressure to shorten sales cycles and bring in the business now.

In my book, 'Selling to Big Companies,' I show sellers what it takes to overcome these roadblocks and get the attention of corporate decision makers today. But salespeople can't do it alone.

'42 Rules for Growing Enterprise Revenue' gives dozens of ideas for turning customer relevance into a company-wide effort. Sales reps want products that deliver on customer needs and are simple to deploy and use in the context of the customer's business. They want the intelligence and awareness that an effective marketing organization provides. They want the extra boost in deal size that comes from selling well thought-out service offerings.

Sales reps need to be able to articulate to partners and customers why their products are a great fit alongside complementary offerings. If their organization doesn't give them what they need, salespeople will improvise. Many do it regularly and well.

But they are more effective if they don't have to make it up as they go along. They are also more efficient if they don't have to spend time re-creating sales tools, messages, and pitches because marketing just didn't get it. When you give them what they need, average salespeople immediately perform at higher levels, and new sales professionals get up to speed much faster.

Sales efforts don't take place in a vacuum. They are accelerated and amplified when the entire company focuses on what matters to customers. When you follow the excellent strategies outlined by Lilia Shirman in '42 Rules for Growing Enterprise Revenue,' that's exactly what will happen.

Jill Konrath
Author, 'Selling to Big Companies'
CEO, SellingtoBigCompanies.com

The concept of customer centricity is over a decade old. In that time, companies have gotten better at tracking customer information, incorporating customer input into product design, and identifying customer needs in their sales and marketing messages. Despite these advances, the most frequent complaint by decision makers involved in complex purchases is that vendors don't listen, don't understand their problems, and don't convincingly articulate value. Something is obviously missing from all that customer-centric activity.

What's missing is context. Most definitions of customer focus center on understanding "customer needs." In practice, that leads to corporate tunnel vision. Marketers zero in on the needs and "pain points" of key audiences, but not on the context within which those needs represent high-value sales opportunities. That may sound like a subtle difference. It's not.

That's because the context, not the need, determines value for both the buyer and the seller. Your relevance to customers starts from understanding needs in context, and your ability to deliver tangible, unique value comes from meeting those needs in a way that fits the context of the customer's business.

'42 Rules for Growing Enterprise Revenue' is about becoming more relevant—about mattering more to the customers and markets that represent the greatest opportunity for growth. Here are numerous integrated, cross-functional initiatives that enable companies to grasp and define the context for revenue opportunities. These rules embody three key themes:

Customer relevance is at the core of any successful growth strategy.
Growth in new markets hinges on targeting the segments in which your product or solution really matters. Expanding in existing markets, whether through deeper account penetration, sales channels diversification, or focusing in on specific industries or audiences, also requires that you prove why you matter. This focus on relevance ensures that customers will value and reward your investments in new growth initiatives.

Being relevant demands cross-functional execution.
This book is not about marketing, or sales, or alliances. It's about initiatives that succeed most spectacularly through cross-functional action and collaboration. Relevance in an enterprise-wide scope encompasses more than product design and marketing message. It includes services and support, channels, sales processes, pricing and packaging—any aspect of business that matters to customers. Marketing can create brilliant programs, deliver well-qualified leads, and produce outstanding "air cover" in the press. Unless that success is accompanied by complementary efforts throughout the organization, the company as a whole cannot reap full benefits.

Sustainable relevance and growth require ongoing innovation and experimentation in every aspect of business.
The rules cover a broad range of strategies because my intent is to encourage companies to examine and experiment with a variety of go-to-market approaches. While some of these strategies will be new to your company, others are reminders to finally implement the commonsense practices you know about, but have yet to carry out.

The rules represent the most effective strategies implemented by B2B companies to increase the relevance and value they deliver in order to drive steep growth curves. The book contains seven sections. The first, Relevance is a Corporate Initiative is about going to market as a single integrated entity rather than a collection of loosely integrated functions, and laying the foundation for relevance throughout the organization. Pursue Markets Where You Matter discusses identifying markets in which you have the potential to deliver the greatest value. Context Defines Relevance and Value, Cultivating Customer Collaboration, Succeeding with Solutions, and Live in Your Customer's Universe discuss approaches for developing, articulating, and delivering benefits that truly matter to customers. Finally, Nurturing Your Channels comes back to one of the most important and oft-neglected factors for successful growth—the ability of the sales channel to comprehend customer needs and context, articulate why you matter, and adapt in sync with the rest of the company.

The ideas in '42 Rules for Growing Enterprise Revenue' have been successfully implemented by leading enterprises including BEA Systems/Oracle, CA, Cisco Systems, Citrix, Informatica, National Oilwell Varco, Symantec, and many others. You will find some of their experiences described in these pages. Use these strategies to experiment and collaborate on similarly successful growth initiatives and to drive relevance, value, and innovation within your business.

Rules Are Meant to Be Broken

Look at the cars, not at the streetlight.

"Hell, there are no rules here—we're trying to accomplish something." - Thomas A. Edison

I often ignore streetlights and jaywalk because I'm in a hurry and eliminating the wait gets me where I'm going faster. The key to not getting run over, of course, is understanding the rules of streetlights—why they exist, what they're meant to accomplish, and how exactly they accomplish it. Once I know that, I can decide intelligently when the rules can be broken to my benefit and with minimal risk.

When I do follow the rules and cross on green, I look around for cars as if there were no streetlights. After all, others might break the rules even while I follow them. By identifying rule breakers early and assessing the threat they pose, I can make an intelligent decision about my own actions.

In business, breaking rules is about leaping ahead. Companies that can trade in the industry standard for a completely new approach can achieve wildly better results than competitors. To do so, you must first understand the rules, or the current best practices and industry stan-dards—when they're useful, what they enable companies to accomplish, and when they needn't apply.

In 'Blue Ocean Strategy,' W. Chan Kim and Renée Mauborgne present a compelling case and some great frameworks for rule-breaking. They teach companies to examine industry assumptions and create completely new models for delivering value, thus ignoring and disrupting the industry's status quo.[i] The "rules" in this book have been proven effective by leading companies, but represent practices that have yet to be adopted by the vast majority of B2B vendors. They represent a break in the rules followed by most companies selling enterprise technology.

There are two ways to use these rules. Put them into practice, or find ways to break them. Either way, focus on the desired outcomes for your company and your customers, rather than on the well-established methods for performing various functions. This is a fundamentally different type of focus. Remember, whether your trip is down a city street or a through a complex business plan, to look at the cars, not at the streetlight. A streetlight has yet to run over anyone.

Part I
Relevance Is a Corporate Initiative

A person's well-being is a combination of a healthy mind, body, emotional state, and spirit. To be truly well is to be well entirely. For a company to be relevant to customers is also to be relevant entirely. Relevance starts with products designed around a specific set of customer needs. Once the product is launched, however, many companies relegate the job or "mattering" to the purview of marketing messages. In fact, the foundation for customer relevance must be present in every aspect of the business, from product to sales and marketing to legal to services. The rules in the first section are about developing the cross-functional collaboration and synchronization required to ensure that you matter to customers at every point in your relationship.

Rule

2

Relevance Is Multidimensional

Place task-specific and broader business needs in context.

What does it mean to matter to customers? Any company with a cent of revenue already provides products and services that address customer needs. Most continue to identify customer needs or pain points as part of their ongoing product management and marketing efforts. But a focus on needs is not enough. As many growing companies have demonstrated, a narrow focus on customer needs may obliterate differentiation, or value, or both.

At high level, all companies need to increase revenue, reduce costs, and retain customers. So many vendors now claim to help with these needs that such claims have become nearly meaningless. Certainly, they are useless as differentiators. At the opposite extreme, all businesses need to accomplish myriad tasks more effectively and efficiently. Vendors often sell product capabilities to fulfill these task-specific needs, without regard for the broader context within which the tasks are taking place. As their market matures and competitors catch up on product features, the focus on task-centered needs exposes the vendor to commoditization and margin degradation. In this situation, both differentiation and value diminish over time.

To matter to enterprise accounts, offer relevant, provable, and unique value and deliver it in the way best suited to the customer's company. That's a much more ambitious mandate than selling products that meet customer requirements. It requires that you place task-specific and broader business needs in context.

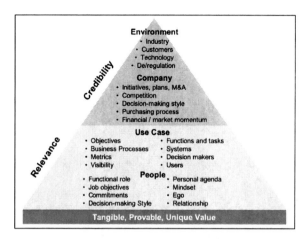

Figure 1: The Context of Enterprise Purchases

The context for enterprise contains at least four layers: the external environment, company situation, use case, and people. Competent sales people know they must understand the first two to gain credibility.

Your customers will hear a recitation of Porter's Five Forces[ii] or similar descriptions of the external environment from every vendor they speak to. They will also hear repeatedly about their own high-level needs as derived from publicly available information on the company's situation and initiatives. Understanding of this level of context is table stakes, required just to be invited to the game.

Your objective, of course, is not simply to be invited into the conversation. To win the deals and deliver value, you need to matter to customers in a unique way. Relevance and perception of value lie in the other two dimensions of context: use cases and people. These determine what aspects of your offerings and relationships matter most, and how customers will assess the value you deliver.

Context should not only define product features and marketing messages, but should guide every aspect of your business. Environment and the company information are useful for more than credibility. Use them to define account micro-segments and guide the customization of everything from pricing models to purchase and support contracts. The context of people and use cases is at the core of defining what you sell, to whom, and how. The rules in the following sections discuss ideas for segmenting markets and audiences and identifying use cases to create greater relevance.

3 Your Organizational Structure Is Irrelevant

Significant impact on growth requires collaboration throughout the organization.

When asked to recall initiatives that had been especially successful, the executives interviewed for this book touched on a common theme: cross-functional teams. Though it seems obvious that any initiative that significantly increases revenue growth requires participation by multiple functions and organizations, many companies still maintain functionally siloed organizations, information, business processes, and mindsets. A functional structure simplifies operations, but creates costly barriers and complexity. Most importantly, it obscures big-picture company objectives. To reach those, what matters is not the org chart, but how employees connect across it.

To encourage collaborative problem-solving and execution, changing the mindset about what constitutes success is the first and most critical step. Employees must be willing and able to take accountability and responsibility to get things done without controlling all the resources required to do it. They need to perceive that their value in the organization stems from their ability to deliver results, not from their scope of control. Though the executive team's observed behavior sets the tone, older and more entrenched cultures will be difficult to shift. If your company is one of these, plan a multi-faceted change effort.

Mark Templeton, the chief executive who has guided Citrix's growth from $500 million to $1.6 billion (and counting), equates the evolution of a company culture to that of an individual's mindset: "Younger people view the material aspects as important, while older people think about the impact they are making." He adds, "Employees need to feel that their importance is based on being a subject matter expert and getting things done, rather than having many direct reports." To change focus from widening control to increasing impact, Citrix is increasing employee training and personal development. Citrix is also encouraging employees to make horizontal moves within the company. Working in different organizations gives them a bigger-picture perspective, and develops relationships across functional lines.

Some companies formalize cross-functional cooperation further. Cisco Systems created councils that spanned business units. The councils met monthly to identify and disseminate best practices from the field to the rest of the company. Large consulting firms often use matrix organizations, where employees belong to multiple industry, geographic, and skill-based communities. These complex matrices work only with clearly prioritized affiliations and guidelines for how to share resources and "credit" for accomplishments.

Pam Fox Rollin, CEO of IdeaShape and an expert in organizational design and team performance, emphasizes that overcoming functional borders requires unwavering commitment from executive leadership. She suggests four levers that promote a cross-functional focus:

- Clarify who has the right and responsibility to make which decisions, and who will be informed, and how, once the decision is made.

- Simplify business processes, and make sure they are well-understood, and easy to adapt to new business needs.

- Provide streamlined, easy routes to access consistent information, without overload.

- Develop collaborative skills and emotional intelligence, which Pam describes as "the crucial last mile," such as surfacing and handling conflict, and understanding and adapting to diverse ways of thinking.

Use new technology to promote and facilitate collaboration. Social networking tools used internally can promote and leverage the skill sets that lie outside employees' functional roles. They provide a conduit for people to share otherwise underutilized knowledge and experience, a forum for building cross-functional communities, and a tool for locating subject matter experts regardless of where they show up on an org chart. Enterprise wikis and social networking and collaboration tools facilitate cross-functional work and information sharing, while drastically reducing email volume and creating re-usable knowledge assets. They also enable cross-functional teams to sprout more frequently and easily, and to be more effective at reaching their objectives and collaborating on whatever matters most to customers.

4 Deposit Your Quarters in Sync

Make sure that departmental and functional efforts are working in concert toward the same goals.

Imagine you are in a room full of Coke machines. Each takes a dollar. You decide you'd like a drink. You pull a handful of quarters out of your pocket, and throw one into a machine. Then you wander over to another machine, and throw in a quarter. You keep drifting around the room, throwing quarters in at random. Getting thirsty? No Cokes to show for all those quarters?

This is obviously an inefficient way to spend your money. Yet many companies drift into this pattern of investment as they grow. Product lines, sales channels, and go-to-market approaches diverge not only from each other, but from what really matters to customers: convenience, simplicity, and a fit for their businesses. Even seemingly clear objectives like revenue targets sometimes get derailed due to a lack of cross-functional alignment. If every organization and every program in your company isn't explicitly focused on the same set of objectives and initiatives, you are wasting your quarters, and your millions, and foregoing the rewards of greater focus.

Citrix accomplished its rapid growth to the $1 billion revenue milestone and beyond by placing all its resources behind a single long-term objective. In 2003, the company was determining its three-year goals, and looking for the right growth strategy. Citrix made the decision to establish $1 billion in annual revenue as the company target, and the X1 initiative was born. Mark Templeton, Citrix CEO, described how the executive team approached the planning task. "We took the future and subtracted the present, and then we needed to figure out what had to change in between." What had to change was the way business was done throughout the company.

To translate the strategic plan into action, the Citrix executive team worked to define how to execute a project that involved everyone in the company. They debated issues including, "What is it like and what are the benefits for individuals to work for a $1 billion company?" and "What would it take within each department to accomplish the $1 billion goal?" The leadership team asked every organization to create a business plan of how to move to the three-year objective. X1 was broken out into smaller objectives that were meticulously measured and tracked.

Creating detailed goals and plans was only the beginning. Every employee had to believe that the objective was attainable, and that they were part of the effort to reach it. To ensure broad executive support and consistency of message, the executive team spent several months defining how to achieve the target. The execs then held countless formal and informal meetings and conversations, communicating that they were on board, and explaining why they supported and believed in X1.

The Citrix example illustrates how critical it is to focus the entire organization around a common goal. Gain consensus among company leadership on both the objectives and methods to pursue them. Without that consensus, you will find orthogonal initiatives that compete rather than reinforce each other. If part of your objective is to become more significant to customers, every person in the organization must understand the context within which your products and services are evaluated, bought, and used, and how their actions fit within that context.[iii] A top-driven focus will ensure that departmental efforts are working in concert toward the same goals. So that, at the end of the day, your company ends up with the most Cokes, and the most quarters.

5 Build Your Portfolio of Corporate Skills

Reinforcing strengths will provide greater rewards than mending weaknesses.

Sustainable growth requires a corporate skill set that is differentiated and relevant to the markets you serve. Your current portfolio of corporate skills includes both strong and lagging capabilities. Some of these skills are must-haves for long-term viability. Some can help you excel in a narrow aspect of your business. A few can create an uncontestable market lead. Manage this portfolio proactively to strengthen core competencies, set consistent objectives, and create guidelines for decision-making and resource allocation. Evaluating the corporate skills portfolio regularly uncovers capabilities that truly matter in your markets, and initiatives with the greatest potential impact on revenue growth.

Corporate skill portfolio management has four stages: identification, assessment, prioritization, and execution.

Identification: Create a list of about ten business attributes that are key to revenue growth. These might include customer loyalty, feature richness or product quality, supply chain efficiency, or the strength of your partnerships. Ask your management team to make lists independently, and then compare. The resulting discussion to narrow the list will undoubtedly be illuminating in itself. This is an opportunity to clarify what is critical to your business and to your customers, and to align the company around the competencies that are most likely to drive growth and profitability.

Assessment: Gauge your company's level of competence in each area. Rate each skill area as lagging, on par with customer expectations, differentiating, or vanguard. The last is on the level of Apple's virtuosity in product design or eBay's market share dominance. Be sure to evaluate your capabilities relative to the broad marketplace, including major competitors, substitutes, new entrants, and leaders in other markets. A wide comparison base normalizes your assessment of strengths: If your highly streamlined supply chain is standard for the industry, for example, then you are simply on par.

Prioritization: Consider how improving your capabilities in each area will accelerate growth. Will raising service quality increase repeat business? Will adding more features to an already competitive product alter customers' choices? Will adding efficiency to your sourcing process spur growth or distract from it? Define the initiatives required to improve your corporate skills and quantify investment and revenue impact for each.

Execution: Incorporate the initiatives you define into your annual business plan. The owner of each initiative will require resources and commitments from multiple organizations. Identify those cross-functional dependencies in the planning phase, so that there are no surprises or finger-pointing later.

This process will identify areas of strength where investment can create long-term competitive advantage. It will also find weaknesses for which you must compensate to protect current market position. Reinforcing strengths will provide greater rewards than mending weaknesses. A University of Wisconsin study found that focusing on errors generates feelings of fatigue, blame, and resistance. Emphasizing what works well and discussing how to get more from strengths taps into creativity, passion, and the desire to succeed.[iv] Teams that examined successes improved twice as much as those that studied mistakes. In their analysis of a massive Gallup Organization study, the authors of 'Now, Discover Your Strengths' also found that the most successful people and organizations play to their strengths, rather than trying to fix weaknesses.[v]

Management of the corporate skill portfolio is an ongoing cycle, not a one-time exercise. While most skills in the portfolio will remain consistent over time, your choices of which to develop will shift year to year. You can't be the vanguard in every aspect of business, and you don't need to. Understanding and developing key strengths can turn them into insurmountable competitive advantages.

A Corporate Skills Portfolio Management Guide and Workbook are available at http://www.shirmangroup.com.

6 Quantum Theory Applies to Business, Too

Planning for alternative outcomes does not have to be a complex statistical exercise.

In the 19th century, scientists believed that the physical laws that ruled the universe were deterministic. Marquis de Laplace, one of the proponents of determinism, argued that if we knew everything about the starting condition, we could use the laws of physics to predict what the universe would be like at any future point in time. Since then, science has moved on to quantum theory. The key realization of quantum theory was that we can never know the condition of our world exactly—not even the exact condition of the tiniest particle. Both the limits of our ability to observe, and the very act of observation, conspire to introduce uncertainty. In other words, we cannot use the laws of physics to precisely predict any future state. The best we can do is to determine the probabilities of a variety of possible future conditions.[vi]

While physicists have abandoned determinism, many business people have not. We manage large, complex organizations. Those organizations are staffed with unpredictable human beings, who create highly complex products and sell to other unpredictable human beings. These transactions take place in an uncertain economic and political climate. Yet few organizations do scenario planning to understand multiple possible outcomes of their strategies. When they do, scenario planning stops with conservative, expected, and aggressive versions of the financial analyses. It rarely extends into operational planning.

Preparing for alternative outcomes does not have to be a complex statistical exercise. Even identifying likely situations at a qualitative level and discussing the subsequent courses of action will help an executive team manage risk and take greater advantage of opportunities.

Scenario planning would have helped one enterprise software company, which acquired a much smaller, highly-successful niche technology vendor in 2004. The new employees received retention packages with vesting in the larger company's stock. Though parts of the two companies were integrated quickly, the sales groups remained separate. Eighteen months after the acquisition, the larger company made the decision to extend the integration to the sales teams, and announced that the smaller company's account managers would become product specialists and join the account teams of the larger company the following quarter. At the two-year anniversary of the acquisition and one quarter after the sales re-org, 65% of the smaller company's sales reps left, taking their expertise and contacts with them. If the company had planned for potential outcomes of the integration, they might have trained additional sales resources on the acquired product, or put in place new retention incentives. The result was a huge loss in sales momentum from which the product never completely recovered.

To avoid such surprises, list the three to five most likely outcomes of major initiatives at the time that a budget allocation occurs. Consider how the possible scenarios will affect your objectives for that initiative. Consider also the impact on other corporate objectives and other organizations. Define specific metrics or early warning signs for each outcome, including who will detect them and how. Agree on what conditions of the warning indicators will merit a response. Finally, sketch out what might be done now or in the future to mitigate or take maximum advantage of the impact of alternative outcomes.

Some companies address uncertainty by putting in place multiple initiatives to accomplish the same goals. Matt Thompson, EVP of World Wide Sales Operations at Adobe, describes this approach as "placing bets." "If you have to grow sales faster than sales expense, you have to keep changing the way you do things. I try strategies that may or may not work. But I always try something new." Matt acknowledges and embraces the uncertainly inherent in business. By trying several new sales initiatives every year, Matt and his team not only reduce the risk associated with the failure of any one strategy, they also learn new techniques and approaches, and become more flexible as an organization.

Part II
Pursue Markets Where You Matter

There are two sources for revenue growth: markets you already serve, and new markets. But what's a market, anyway? At its simplest, the Wikipedia definition describes a market as "any structure that allows buyers and sellers to exchange any type of goods, services, and information." This explanation doesn't help us find places to grow nor understand why we uniquely matter to the market participants. In practice, we talk about markets in terms of customer segments, product categories, or geographic regions. Unfortunately, these definitions are too broad to guide effective, customer-centric strategy. They fail to provide enough insight into our audiences, and leave us to create generic marketing and sales approaches and tactics that look and sound too similar to everyone else's. The rules in this section present additional ways to define markets and segment audiences. These alternate views facilitate the design of actionable go-to-market strategies that improve both market reach and customer relevance.

7 Size Matters, and So Does Ability

Whether success in a new market is "doable" for your company is as important as any market characteristic.

When prioritizing growth initiatives, many companies focus too much on the size of a market opportunity, and insufficiently on their ability to successfully pursue it. Their business plans analyze opportunity size, the rate of revenue growth, and market share potential. The revenue opportunity is quantified by customer segment, geography, and product. Risk assessments focus on external factors like competitors, regulators, and customers, even though most new strategies fail due to internal issues.

In selecting target markets, balance enthusiasm about the opportunity with a realistic assessment of your company's ability to execute. Can you be uniquely relevant and create, communicate, and deliver differentiated value? Will the capabilities you develop be useful in the long term? Constantinos Markides, a professor of Strategic Leadership at London Business School, comments that in evaluating diversification opportunities, "like good chess players, forward-thinking managers will be thinking two or three moves ahead."[vii]

"It's all about execution, and there are not that many companies that have execution as a discipline," commented Chris Cook, now EVP and General Manager of CA's Application Performance Management Business Unit. Chris came to CA through the acquisition of Wily Technology, one of the most successful investments in CA history. Since its inception, Wily made execution the central factor in planning growth. The management team translated each revenue objective into specific execution plans. Chris recalls, "We thought about the details of how we are going to deliver the number. Via which channel, and how much sales do we need per sales rep? How do these numbers match history? Is it doable?"

That simple question—whether success in a new market is "doable" for your company—is as important as any market characteristic. New products and markets take a toll on sales execution. Before committing to a new strategy, anticipate the changes that will be required of the sales process. Changes like longer sales cycles, increased partner involvement, or greater complexity of product mix are likely to cause big disruptions. Existing sales compensation and the momentum of existing products and practices will make such adjustments difficult and possibly unwelcome. Consider your sales practices and compensation model carefully and plan for changes that will encourage behaviors appropriate to the new market.

Consider also the number of new skills reps will need in order to articulate relevance and value of new offerings or engage new buyers. Existing channel partners and service and support personnel will also need new tools and education. In many cases, you many need to recruit new reps or channel partners with different expertise or within new geographies, and in-region resources deployed to support them. Though entry into a new market does not necessarily involve new products, success will lead to demand for new or modified product features or implementation and service processes. Make sure product management, R&D, and Services groups are prepared to add at least some of these changes to their roadmap. Get agreement and allocate dollars to these areas proactively. A realistic assessment and investment now will prevent unmet expectations, firefighting, and finger-pointing later.

Assessing Opportunity	Assessing Ability to Execute
• Size of the addressable market • Growth rates for your product/service category in the target market • Competitive pressure • Customer demands • Potential revenue from deeper penetration of existing accounts • Potential revenue from expansion into new accounts • Foreseeable external changes that may spur demand	• Sales alignment and acceptance • Relevant sales skills and domain expertise • Ability to leverage partnerships • Marketing domain expertise • Success of pilot deployments or programs • Expertise and skill-sets of service and support organizations • Existing relationships with relevant thought leaders • Proven record of successful acquisitions, if required to enter new market

Figure 2: Balancing Opportunity Size with Ability to Execute

8 Markets Are Audiences and Needs

To accurately size the addressable opportunity, look at the intersection of needs and audiences.

The word "market" is used to describe different aspects of an opportunity. We think about geographies, product categories, target buyer groups, and combinations of these as markets.[viii] To clearly assess an opportunity and define actionable strategy to pursue it, be clear about what "market" you're really after.

Though markets are often defined in terms of product categories, what really creates a market is a need. Mobile phones met the need for mobile communication that had previously been addressed by phone booths. Of course, mobile phones also meet the need for communication in general. As a result, fixed-line voice revenue is declining and fixed-line service is slowly following the phone booth into oblivion. Once a need is met by another product category, the market for the old category disappears. The market to address the need remains, and often expands. Companies like MCI that identified too strongly with the product category (fixed-line telephone networks), rather than with the need (communication), have found themselves in dire straits. Kodak is facing a similar fate. The company identified so strongly with the film camera market that it was unable to move quickly into the digital photography category, despite internal analysis showing that the need to record experiences would soon be met entirely without film.

We also define "market" in terms of groups of buyers, as in, "the North American market" or "the small and medium business market." Categorizing audiences provides insight into needs, and can guide definition of product roadmaps and go-to-market strategy (Rule 9). To accurately size the addressable opportunity, look at the intersection of needs and audiences.

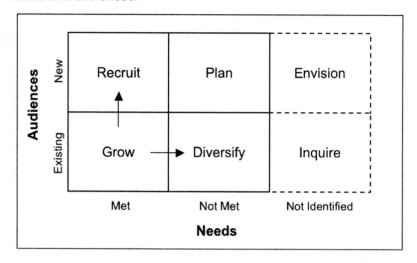

Figure 3: Markets as Intersections of Audiences and Needs

There are growth opportunities in every region of the Audience-Needs matrix, but the strategies for pursuing them are very different. Growing sales to your existing customers by better meeting a consistent set of needs is likely to involve tactics such as cross-selling and up-selling that raise revenue per customer. You might introduce product or service enhancements, but all new offerings will closely relate to those you sell already. To meet different needs of your existing customers will likely require new lines of business. Recruiting new customers who have the same needs as those you already serve places an emphasis on sales and marketing rather than on new product development. The competitors you face in each quadrant may be different as well. To find and pursue the most relevant growth opportunities, evaluate the intersections of needs and audiences in terms of both the size of the opportunity, and your company's ability to execute (see Rule 4).

There is less risk in moving one step at a time, rather than jumping simultaneously into addressing needs you have not met before for target buyers to whom you have never sold. When introducing new products in the same category as your existing offerings, evaluate whether they are truly complementary—that is, whether they address a common need or audience.

9 Slice and Dice Your Market

Use segment characteristics to determine your go-to-market approach.

I once worked with a manufacturing manager whose "hobby" was chemistry. A chemical engineer by training, Mike had set up a lab in his garage where he used common household chemicals to develop better cleaners, polishers, and glue and label removers. Buying the inexpensive chemical mixes in bulk, Mike targeted his cleaners for very specific applications. There was a "bicycle cleaner," packaged in small 4 oz. bottles that Mike sold to biking enthusiasts through specialty bicycle shops. A motorcycle cleaner had different packaging, different distribution, and of course, a different buyer. Cleaners for cars and shop tools each had an audience. Another words, Mike used the classic consumer goods approach of focusing on audiences and how they bought and used the product—not on the product itself.

Despite the seeming importance of segmentation to marketing, the amount of segmentation done by most B2B vendors is surprisingly small. Company size and geography are often the only criteria for segmentation, with industry being a distant third. Even when the segmentation is used for organizing the sales channel, or for making packaging and pricing decisions, customer characteristics rarely drive decisions in other areas.

Reveal new revenue opportunities by segmenting your target customer base in new ways. Some possible segmentation criteria are:

- **Customer attitudes:** These relate to how companies do business, make decisions, and might include tolerance for risk, or speed of technology adoption.

- **Experience with you:** Familiarity and experience with your company and product is a key segmentation criteria. The next rule drills down on segmenting relationships.

- **Objectives or Use cases:** Customers in the same industry or with similar business models might face similar problems, and may look to you for similar reasons. Think about specific situations, business processes, or goals that they may share. (See Rule 34.)

- **Audiences:** Define audiences based on their roles and responsibilities within an organization or within the decision-making process.

Use segment characteristics to determine your go-to-market approach. Having defined groups of companies with similar needs, and identified specific audiences within these target accounts, set specific objectives for each segment. If your goal is to expand within multinational accounts where you have a limited presence in a single geographic area, you may decide to partner with local resellers to expand into foreign divisions of a group of core accounts. If you want to engage particular audiences or types of buyers, target value propositions, communication channels, and sales techniques to them. To expand into new uses of your products, define campaigns, solutions, and services that cater to each type of use. If you decide to raise deal size or change the product mix within a segment, you might implement sales spiffs to drive sales reps towards specific types of deals.

Your objectives in each segment can drive vastly different positioning, marketing programs, and sales strategy. The possibilities are endless, but understanding exactly what you're trying to accomplish and with which customers will help guide efficient marketing and sales support expenditure.

Of course, to do segmentation and measure the effectiveness of targeted strategies, you need to be able to measure by segment. Chances are, however, your systems are not set up to do so. In truth, even "back of the envelope" analysis can guide initial segment-based efforts. Don't let sluggish IT change processes data become an excuse for inaction. I was amazed to see a 10-person industry marketing team at a multi-billion dollar technology company struggling to report on revenue and customer satisfaction scores by industry. The group of very knowledgeable experts was extracting satisfaction and revenue numbers manually from sales data. While this was wasteful and far from ideal, the team was producing an estimated $120 million in business by focusing attention on specific segments.

10 Know How Well They Know You

Revenue per account should be accompanied by other quantitative and qualitative objectives.

Customers' experience and depth of relationship with your company are critical factors in determining sales strategy and marketing plans. Green-field, new, and well-established accounts need different amounts of education, marketing tools, sales processes, and types of support. Good sales reps adjust their in-account activity based on their customers' past spending. Support this approach with proactive programs that uphold and complement the reps' individual efforts.

Start by segmenting accounts into revenue categories meaningful to your business. Though actual spend levels will be unique to your company, the following relationship categories provide useful qualitative descriptions.

Strategic Accounts have standardized on your offerings to meet a specific need across their operations. They consistently make large investments, and C-level sponsors consider you the go-to vendor. Ideally, these accounts see you as a partner and your account manager as a domain expert.

Core Accounts use your offerings across multiple organizations, geographies, or business processes. They spend regularly, but your share of wallet here is lower than at strategic accounts. Your rep has good relationships with functional or department leads and senior managers, but doesn't always hear about opportunities while needs are still being formulated. Some departments or executives are loyal to competitors.

Beach Head Accounts have made one or several small purchases but are yet to make a major investment. Your sales rep has some relationships at the mid-management level, but little or no access to senior decision makers. You hear about most opportunities after the requirements are well defined.

Green Field Accounts have not bought from you in the last three years. The contacts you have in your database may be out-of-date or not your target buyers.

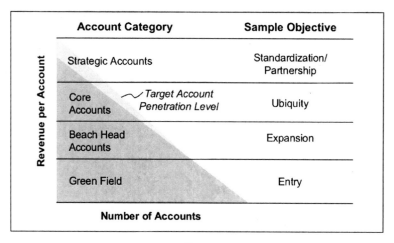

Account Category   **Sample Objective**

Revenue per Account

Strategic Accounts   Standardization/
                                  Partnership

Core   ∿ Target Account
Accounts   Penetration Level   Ubiquity

Beach Head   Expansion
Accounts

Green Field   Entry

Number of Accounts

Figure 4: Sample Account Relationship Categories and Objectives

Determine your objectives for each group to capture its untapped revenue. Figure 4 illustrates a sample set of expansion strategies, targeting a shift to greater account penetration. For strategic accounts that see you as a best-of-breed vendor, a broader relationship as a trusted advisor is a good next-step objective. Core accounts may be ready for enterprise-wide agreements and deeper relationship-building with senior decision makers.

Complement revenue goals with other quantitative and qualitative objectives. Include goals for relationships, referenceability, average deal size, or breadth of presence. If you've been doing small deals in your beach head accounts, consider setting an objective for higher average sales. If you're present in only one geography or functional area among your core accounts, identify one or two other areas you need to penetrate within the next year.

If your sales reps or channel partners are doing good account planning, some may have set such objectives and already have plans in place to accomplish them. Ensure that such planning is universal, and that the execution is repeatable across account segments, and across sales reps. Define marketing and services initiatives that support segment goals. Track contacts and internal references so that your company can make full use of your account relationships and the customer's past experiences, even as reps come and go.

Rule

11 Customers Are People, not Segments

Inform stakeholders about how the purchase will affect their day-to-day jobs.

Go to a modern animated children's movie, and you're sure to find lots of jokes, symbols, and even entire subplots that are completely incomprehensible to the preschoolers. They're there for the adults, who are the financial decision makers and end-users of the movie. The film-makers are acting on a concept that many B2B vendors underutilize: There are multiple constituencies involved in the purchase and consumption of a product, and you have to cater to all of them.

You've carefully segmented your target market, and identified the kinds of companies most likely to buy from you. That's an important step in focusing resources and defining go-to-market strategy. But segments, industries, and geographies don't make purchase decisions. Neither do companies. People use products, contact support, and recommend vendors. People make purchase decisions. They do all this with both company objectives and their own personal interests in mind.

Erik Frieberg, a seasoned Silicon Valley marketing executive, described a corner-turning experience at Escalate—one of the first online e-commerce companies. Escalate was pursuing a big opportunity with a big-name customer, Williams-Sonoma. At the first, hard-won customer meeting, the rep discovered a surprisingly large variety of people in the room. There were sales and marketing people with lead generation objectives, and the Director of

Customer Service wondering how to simplify customer support. There were merchandise managers concerned about how to showcase products, and web developers evaluating the technology. The pitch that had been prepared by marketing didn't begin to address such diverse priorities. Instead the rep focused on each individual in turn. It worked, and Escalate adopted what is now called "audience marketing." The change helped Escalate break into new accounts and shorten sales cycles.

Nothing beats face-to-face interaction with real customers and real users to build awareness of customers as individuals rather than segments or accounts. Override sales' desire to "protect" their accounts, and insist that engineers, support personnel, and marketing staff visit customers. Ask them to observe what happens day-to-day, and to interact freely with the people they are observing. This first-hand exposure will reveal both the business and personal interests of the people who influence whether and how your products and services are used.

The currently popular term "audience marketing" is unfortunate. It implies that the focus on individual needs stops at messaging. Consider how product design, the sales process, financial terms, and after-sales services or support meet individual needs of various stakeholders. Help buyers and end-users understand how they, specifically, will interact with the product and with your company. Inform stakeholders about how the purchase will affect their day-to-day jobs.

Introscope™, a technically complex product from CA, monitors the details deep within applications in order to identify potential performance issues. There is an interface for system administrators, and one for IT system managers that pinpoints problems. But these are not the only constituencies, and they don't hold the purse-strings to software budgets. Because the systems that Introscope monitors are often mission-critical, business managers also want to know that all is well. So CA summarizes performance at different levels of detail, including via high-level dashboards for business people. CA also has sales and marketing tools for a wide range of people involved in purchase decisions. Whether a CA sales rep meets with a developer, a system admin, or the VP of customer service, they have both the story and the product view for each one.

Catering to individual needs and interests is especially critical when selling into a flat organization because each person is likely to have a bigger steak in the purchase decision, and a greater influence on it. Understanding the perspective of each stakeholder speeds up the sales process, but it also speeds up adoption and acceptance after the purchase is made. This in turn accelerates the benefits the customer gets from the product.

12 Commit to Long Stays Abroad

Growth in foreign markets takes time, patience, and help from the locals.

Foreign and developing markets provide one of the greatest opportunities for revenue growth. Entire categories of products may not yet be available. In other cases, such as communication, the market may be more advanced and ready for mass adoption of leading-edge products.

Though there is ample data available on growth rates, market sizes, and the social, political, and economic stability in the region, desktop research cannot replace an on-location evaluation. Unless you plan to license your product or service to a local company, success abroad requires an intimate understanding of individual country markets. Many companies segment the world into regions: EMEA, APAC, and the Americas. In truth, the countries within these geographies are so diverse that the only practical way to pursue them is individually. If you already have a presence in a region, encourage your on-location staff to contribute country-specific data to the planning process. Break down your regional marketing or sales plans into country plans.

If you do not yet have a presence in a specific country, gather insights from both locals and foreigners already conducting business in that country. Investigate the unique challenges that local customers and foreign companies encounter in the market, and be prepared to address them. Evaluate whether the cultural norms of doing business there align with your company's values. Business success in some markets may involve bribery, disregard for environmental protections, or labor practices you would never contemplate in the home office. Decide how flexible you're willing to be, and determine how holding to your company's values will affect your ability to succeed in these markets.

Look first at the low hanging fruit. Countries with a common language and no requirement to "localize" products and documentation require smaller initial investment. International accounts are also a good launching-off point. Use these references in other parts of the world where your existing customers have a strong presence. You can also leverage the added credibility of internal references within an international account to sell into these customers' foreign divisions.

Growth in foreign markets takes time, patience, and help from the locals. Before entering a new market, amass the right resources and internal support required for a long-term commitment. Pulling out of a market because early results don't meet expectations damages credibility immensely. Potential customers lose trust in your commitment to the area, and partners view any investment in an alliance as fraught with risk. To re-enter the same country later will be even more complicated than the first time, as you fight to overcome distrust.

Many companies that expand globally are public and therefore driven by quarterly results. Despite the best intentions, board or investor pressure can override early good intentions to give the new country time to succeed. In overseas markets, you'll need to foster relationships and cultivate business networks. These take time and patience. Salesforce.com, which revolutionized enterprise software with its *software as a service* model, understands patience. The company now has a highly successful and lucrative business in Japan, but it took five years after entering that market to see the large return on investment. "If you're harvesting revenue in a tactical or opportunistic way, the success tends to be short lived," commented Jeremy Cooper, VP of Corporate Marketing at Salesforce.com who helped Siebel, Oracle, and most recently Salesforce.com strengthen their presence in Asia.

To ensure long-term success in foreign markets, invest in the development of a skilled local staff, and in long-term relationships. Be prepared to make broad investments well ahead of measurable impact on revenue. By demonstrating patience early, you can create a foundation for long-term growth abroad.

Mix with the Locals

Even with the best partners, local employees are critical to success abroad.

In North America, you can sell almost entirely on value (Rules 26–29). In most other markets, relationships come first, and business second. The low-tech, high-touch business conducted in most of the world relies on pre-existing relationships. As any company with offices abroad knows, in-country presence and partners are indispensable to local relevance.

Partners can handle everything from sales and distribution to deployment and customer service. As with all alliances, such partnerships require commitment to a joint business plan with clear accountability and metrics. Start with building relationships and articulating how the partner organization will benefit from the relationship. Create rules of engagement and define timelines for investment and progress. Less structured relationships where the local partner views little commitment or investment are likely to yield disappointing results.

When you engage with local partners, determine what the partner can and cannot deliver and how you plan to compensate them. An agent helps establish relationships and make sales introductions, and gets paid referral fees for specific contacts or transactions. Working with them can help you gain entrée into customers and partners you may not have been able to access yourself. When Datap was expanding from North America into Europe and Africa, it benefitted immensely from working with local agents. The company's ability to break into a tough Middle Eastern market is a great example of the power of local partners, and the need to find the right ones. CrossKeys was targeting the oil and gas industry in Saudi Arabia, and doing all the things recommended by embassies and trade publications. Unfortunately, they were unable to build the needed connections with buyers. Finally, the company hired a local, well-connected agent who had already worked with the target customer. The agent accomplished in a few weeks what might have taken years of business development and sales efforts.

Other types of partners require deeper, longer-term commitments. A reseller takes greater responsibility for ongoing sales and customer relationships than does an agent, and is rewarded through a reseller discount. A total solution provider often resells, but may also refer or influence sales made directly by you. They receive a combination of reseller discounts and referral or influence fees.

Even with the best partners, local employees are critical to success abroad. To show commitment to the area, establish local offices staffed with local people speaking the local language. They know the culture intimately and have the connections you need. "Decide whether you want to be Co. Japan, or Co. IN Japan" advises Jeremy Cooper of Salesforce.com. When Salesforce.com expanded into Japan, the company faced an especially difficult challenge in balancing local representation with company knowhow. Salesforce.com's unique new technology delivery model of software as a service required a new approach. Even experienced sales people would need the support of managers with tenure and experience in the company. Salesforce.com found talented local resources and used the expat staff to transfer skills and knowledge. The early interaction among expats and locals created long-term relationships that foster collaboration between the region and headquarters.

Local presence from headquarters is required to recruit local employees and pass on critical product and company information. Their early presence also helps bring knowledge of foreign markets back to corporate when the expats return to headquarters. Over time, as local staff takes over the day-to-day management and execution, they will also need greater autonomy to adapt sales, marketing, and alliance approaches to the market. Even so, management must be committed to regular visits to field offices in order to observe local needs first hand. Visits by executives from headquarters are also invaluable in demonstrating the importance of international accounts, and for building relationships by mixing with the locals.

Part III
Cultivate Customer Collaboration

When customer relationship management (CRM) gained attention in the 1980's, it was a technology category. Over time, CRM matured into a set of business practices and attitudes. Today, we are seeing a similar wave of innovation in technology and the way businesses relate to customers.[ix] This one is called 2.0. While the landscape of 2.0 communities and technologies is still young and evolving rapidly, its impact on customer expectations is already emerging. Customers demand greater vendor transparency and increased influence over what is sold to them, where, and how. They also exercise greater collective and individual power in the marketplace.

The new mindset will not be constrained to online interaction or to B2C markets. Just as with CRM, corporations will need to adapt new mindsets and processes to engage customers interactively and collaboratively. B2B companies that can redefine the customer relationship from one of buyer-seller to that of a team collaborating to design a solution will command greater loyalty and higher average prices. The tools to do so are available now. The following rules focus on the mindset and practices that make customer collaboration possible with or without IT investment.

14 Relationships Happen Between Contract Renewals

Create a process that touches customers with relevant ideas that are neither sales pitches nor marketing campaigns.

To communicate a credible value proposition, you need to understand your customer's business. To deliver value, you must be committed to your customer's success. Unfortunately, the structure of most businesses supports the former more than the latter. Enterprise sales reps get compensated for closing big deals. Once the deal is closed, the rep moves on to the next account, to return in a year, or two, or three, when it's time to renew the contract.

If Sales doesn't touch the customer between sales cycles, and Support only does so when the customer asks for help, then who is really managing the relationships with your top accounts? What happens to customer relationships between contract renewals?

Chapman Kelly is a leader in health care compliance and cost-containment services for Fortune 500 companies. Michael Browning, Director of Strategic Development, described the processes his company has put in place to prevent voids and dips in customer relationships. The company understood early that not all customer contact is created equal. Simply sending an email or calling on the telephone and saying hello or "checking in" does not provide the customer with value or develop greater trust. "We want the information to be useful and valuable—this makes it about the customer. We try to take the customers' point of view, and figure out what would be valuable to them," explained Michael. Chapman Kelly makes sure that contacts and communication are educational and useful, and that interactions help build the company's reputation as a subject matter expert that can help solve problems.

Michael helps his sales force create such interactions by giving sales people good reasons to stay in touch with clients during the downtime between project completion and the time when clients are ready to buy again. To create content that will be valuable to customers, Chapman Kelly asks its services organization and business development people to create articles based on real deployments. The small business development staff, made up of people who understand both sales and marketing, uses Google alerts and keyword searches on target industries and customers to provide a constantly-updated sales toolbox with timely discussion topics and articles. The company also created a system that reminds sales people to contact customers based on pre-set time intervals or milestones within ongoing projects. Sales reps always have relevant and interesting content to present. The support is not limited to direct reps. Brokers also get information they can use with clients, and even brand as their own.

The result of such ongoing relationship management is a completely transformed sales process. "Many times if we're able to form a close relationship with the client, the competitive RFP process is not even necessary. If the client is required or prefers to issue a competitive RFP, our position means we can help define the RFP and suggest criteria, questions, or requirements that our competitors may have a difficult time meeting," commented Michael.

Don't leave the task of creating an ongoing dialogue to sales reps. They focus on the next big deal, and often lack the time to figure out and use complex news services, or to seek out and deliver information to customers without immediate sales opportunities. Create a process that touches customers with relevant ideas that are neither sales pitches nor marketing campaigns, but rather relevant and timely resources for their business.

15 Hand the Pen to the Customer

Give customers a chance to weigh in before you write a single word of messaging.

If your customers aren't creating your messaging, it's probably wrong. Consumer companies spend millions on gauging customer reactions to everything from logos and ads to products and packaging. Catalogs test direct mailers, websites test minute details of page layout, button text, and color scheme, and toy companies gather toddlers into a room to watch them play. Companies selling to other businesses would do well to learn from their B2C cousins.

Here's what happens when the customer is not involved. This is an actual "elevator pitch" seen online, as posted by a sales manager: (Name of manager and company to remain anonymous to protect the guilty). "[Vendor] solutions give companies the ability to increase revenues and profits using a standardized approach, with quick implementation and substantially lower risk and price than alternative solutions." This was the entire statement—no additional information. Do you have any idea what they're selling? Tempted to find out? The claims are so generic and vague, I doubt many potential customers would be. This pitch fails to mention what is being sold, and claims rather than demonstrates value. Had the writer of this pitch asked for customer input, they would have discovered which details could validate their claims and better engage the target audience.

Am I suggesting you write your messaging and then get feedback from customers? Not exactly. Once you've defined your value propositions and written the messaging, its too late to get input. At that point, you will be less able and willing to hear the polite and subtle criticism that you're likely to get from customer looking at completed messages.

Instead of getting feedback, hand the customer the pen at the beginning of the process. The Application Performance Management division of CA found its deals bogged down at the budget justification stage. They had to find a way to demonstrate that the payback for the purchase was well worth the price. Though there were already some great success stories about past deployments, the marketing team realized they needed a more universal approach to demonstrate how their company delivered value. The team decided to ask customers what benefits they were deriving from use of CA products. CA interviewed ten customers, and also spoke to several partners. The interviewers captured both qualitative and quantitative benefits. The value proposition, messaging, and ROI estimates were developed using the information and direct quotes gathered from customers. The team then returned to those same customers and several others to confirm that the method of demonstrating value was valid. The new messaging has been extremely effective in engaging customers, and has enabled the sales team to engage more senior decision makers with greater confidence.

There are other ways to ask customers to contribute to your messaging. If you conduct an annual survey, include open-ended questions about the value customers have received, and would like to receive in the future from your company. Ask your customer advisory council to articulate in their own words why they chose your product or service.

By giving customers a chance to weigh in before you write a single word of messaging, you:

- Learn to speak the customers' language in describing their challenges and their results.
- Create a value proposition that rings true for other customers in the same segment.
- Find real, referenceable proof points for your claims.

Of course, the open-ended conversations have the added benefit of giving you the opportunity to listen, learn, and build relationships with your customers. The conversations also give you the chance to identify additional ways to create value.

16 Stop Marketing, Start Collaborating

You don't need to dive into an ocean of social media and networking tools in order to have conversations.

There are now so many channels for communication, it seems customers should be more engaged than ever. *Are yours?* If not, or if not enough, take a look at how much time your marketing people spend on outbound messages, and how much on creating and participating in conversations with customers.

Your customers are participating in social networking and contributing to social media. MyBlogLog.com, a site that attempts to consolidate data across multiple communities lists 55 social media services. LinkedIn, Twitter, Technorati, Digg, Plaxo, a sea of blogging platforms...new ones pop up almost daily. Find out which your customers frequent, and design a process for participating in those.

The good news is you don't need to dive into an ocean of social media and networking tools in order to have conversations. Here are some ideas for making some traditional marketing methods more interactive.

Collateral and White Papers - Create a Wiki instead of static product data sheets, brochures, and white papers. Provide a framework and some base content, then give your customers the ability to contribute. You can moderate to ensure accuracy, of course. You'll have more complete information, on topics that are relevant to your audience. Best of all, the information will be more trusted, and customers will feel ownership for what's there.

Websites - Don't hide customer feedback and support in a corner of your site. Place feature request and comment links right on product pages, so that customers can respond immediately to the content they see. Asking a question gets the customer more engaged than downloading a white paper. Involve product management and engineering in responding to the queries. It's a great way to for them to touch the customers they otherwise rarely or never see. Post the most interesting questions and answers or turn them into additional content.

Press Releases - What if your PR people became your customers' and partners' PR people? Lots of stories would best be told by someone other than a vendor. Having customers as narrator would also make the stories more likely to get picked up for coverage. Give your PR group the assignment to build relationships with customers' and partners' PR staffs, in addition to the press and analysts. Rather than writing every story, your PR staff can then assist partners and customers with replying to PR opportunities.

Webinars - By now, webinars are a "traditional" marketing tool. Many companies tend to make webinars broadcasts rather than conversations. Be sure to use interactive tools. Select the webinar hosting services that offer polls, chat, and Q&A. Use surveys both before and after your webinars. And don't limit the surveys to "Did you find this useful?" Ask questions that help you understand customers. Ask questions that customers will be interested in too, and then share the results either during the webinar, or as a value-added follow-up.

In-person Events - These are expensive, so why spend the entire time lecturing on information that's already in your collateral? Third-party presenters can be more interesting, but any lecture can get dreary fast. Give attendees lots of time to interact with you and with each other, while you listen and take notes. Consider a workshop rather than a presentation format so that the entire event is interactive.

If opening a conversation with customers seems too fraught with risk, try letting a small group of customers you know well contribute, then open further when you're comfortable managing a broader conversation.

17 Turn Your Pitch into a Conversation

Script the sales presentation with questions and discussion points instead of a spiel.

Imagine meeting someone at a cocktail party. In the first minute of small talk, you discover that the new acquaintance wants to work for your company and in your functional area. They proceed to rattle off their age, IQ, weight, height, and the list of companies they've worked for. They mention they have two dogs and a house in Vail, then set off on a detailed description of their education and skills, and how these are a great match for your company. The only reason you are still there, of course, is because they've managed to corner you.

Sound ridiculous? Yet many corporate presentations are exactly like this. The first slides give company background. Then comes the customer logo slide that some poor marketing associate spent hours arranging. Then a description of how increased competition, more demanding customers, changing regulation, and new technology are creating pressure to cut costs, grow revenue, and become more responsive to customers. Next is a diagram of functions and capabilities that the customer needs, followed by the "marchetecture"—the same diagram filled in with product names to match each need. The next 20 slides describe functions in detail, complete with lists of features and benefits. At the very end are case studies that prove how useful the product is to real customers. By now, however, the audience is bored and wishing they'd begged out of the meeting and gotten a summary from someone else.

Experienced sales people will re-arrange this presentation. They will incorporate information about the customer that they've been able to unearth prior to their meeting. Still, the presentation slides handicap sales with a flawed approach, rather than arming them with a compelling story and the tools to lead an engaging dialogue.

Instead of giving reps another new and improved PowerPoint presentation, give them a conversation. Specifically, create a white board talk guide. Include a progression of simple drawings or diagrams that the rep can reproduce on any whiteboard or napkin. Script it with questions and discussion points instead of a spiel. Suggest different paths for the rep to take depending on where the discussion leads. By removing the canned slides and allowing reps to present information apparently impromptu, you give your sales people enormous credibility and flexibility. The result is a conversation where customers contribute ideas, and the content evolves based on the here-and-now in the room, and not what marketing thought up a month ago back at headquarters.

To make the discussion truly engaging, start the script with questions. Teach reps to actively listen and play back information they are hearing from the customers. Use role playing to help reps learn to prolong the time they are willing to spend on listening before jumping into the presentation. Once they do start their white board presentation, "script in" opportunities to listen more. Provide at least a few instances where the presenter encourages the customer to pick up a pen and contribute to the evolving drawing.

The impact of such participation is to transform an informational meeting into a collaborative brainstorming session. It places reps and customers on the same side of the table, designing a solution together. The rep is likely to walk away with more information about the account, and leave behind a sense that he's already provided something valuable.

Ask Customers to Say "I Wish"

Foster opportunities for unexpected discoveries.

"I wish" are the most powerful words one can hear from a customer. I was once interviewing a client's customers in order to quantify the benefits they were receiving from the company's products. Direct access to customers is difficult to arrange, so I used the rare opportunity to gather additional information. I asked a very simple question: "What can we do to help you get more value from our products?" Several customers mentioned they wanted the company to prolong their commitment to customer success through a new post-sale service offering. This discovery was unexpected, un-planned, and pointed to a completely new revenue opportunity for my client.

Foster opportunities for unexpected discoveries. Ask questions about how you can increase the value of your offerings, such as, "Is there something you wish we could do to help you ac-complish more with our products?" or "How can we help you create all the value you hoped to get from this purchase?" Inquiring about customers' wishes or hopes with a focus on value elicits topics that truly matter to their business, and uncovers value that customers will reward with loyalty and continued purchases. It also moves the conversation away from their current image and expectations about your company. Asking for wishes requests a flight of the imagination. You will hear feedback about your existing solution, but you're just as likely to get ideas about complementary products, services, or practices. Use these to add depth and value to your offerings.

National Oilwell Varco (NOV), the leading provider of oilfield products and services, routinely asks customers to make wishes. NOV recently launched a spectacularly successful solution based on customer input. In their discussions with customers, NOV sales reps and executives regularly inquire about customers' needs and plans. These discussions uncovered customers' desire to focus on their core competencies of drilling for oil, rather than on purchasing and inventory management. Leveraging its supply chain expertise, NOV created an innovative solution. The NOV RigStore™ places supplies directly on the offshore rigs. NOV manages and owns the inventory, and the customer simply purchases needed items on-site. No requisitions, no inventory, no obsolescence. The NOV RigStore initiative maximizes revenue by capturing the vast majority of that oil rig's spend. By asking customers to wish, NOV found a way to grow revenue and create important benefits for its customers.

If most of your customer interactions are focused on sales, you may well miss such open-minded thinking. Create opportunities for interaction that are not tied to a sales or marketing objective. Amdocs, the leading provider of business systems for the communications industry, listens to customers in a variety of ways and at every level in its organization. The CEO and executive staff meet annually with the customer advisory board made up of executives from top accounts. The CTO and product line heads meet with a technical advisory board of 30 to 40 customer technology leaders twice per year. The company's strategic reference program includes networking opportunities with reference accounts. Amdocs also collects quantitative data in a formal customer satisfaction survey. In addition, to ensure undiluted information about user needs and wants, Amdocs exposes the development team to end-users. Engineers who design call center software, for example, sit next to call center reps and watch them use the product. Rule 15 lists additional ways to create forums for interaction that will allow you to solicit customer wishes.

Of course, just gathering information isn't enough. To ensure the intelligence gets disseminated into your company, plan quarterly debriefs with those who've had the opportunity to hear customers' wishes. Use these meetings to identify repeating themes and assign an owner to investigate if and how you can make those wishes reality. If your systems allow, correlate anecdotal and systematic data gathering to prioritize investments.

19 Relevant References Are Farmed, Not Hunted

Use the reference program to provide value to customers.

Obtaining references can be a series of rushed searches for testimonials and quotes, or a systematic process for cultivating customer validation and evangelism. Increase the applicability and value of references through a repeatable process that engages customers as active participants, not passive sources of "sign-offs."

A program allows your company to farm rather than hunt for references. "Lack of a program creates a dull pain in every area, and a broad productivity hit," commented Holly Lugassy, who has run reference programs at BEA, Borland, and Adobe Systems. Without a program, a fire drill ensues every time marketing or sales needs a reference. This places revenue at risk and supplies the most available, rather than the most relevant, references. Ad-hoc reference searches also overtax supportive accounts. "The result," commented Holly, "is customer and organizational burnout."

The reference program should encompass every form of customer validation you may need, from quotes to video testimonials to private calls with other customers. Even accounts that shun public statements can support you in valuable ways. There are three primary uses of customer references:

Market Awareness: Stories or quotes you use in press releases and with analysts create market awareness and credibility, as do customers blogs and conference presentations. Phone interviews with press and analysts, either public or under NDA, also broaden market awareness.

Deal Support: Create tools for the entire sales cycle. "Elevator stories" can be named or anonymous, but no longer than 90 seconds. They describe the company, its objectives and challenges, what you did, and the resulting benefits. Reps should be able to recite these as they initially engage prospects. Success stories in collateral, websites, and presentations are for the discovery stage. Detailed financial benefit and technical descriptions of deployments, and customers-to-customer calls help build business cases and support prospects' due diligence process.

Sales Enablement and Motivation: References have a second audience—your sales channels. When reps and channel partners can easily access reference materials for the entire sales cycle, their own confidence rises. Maintain a categorized index of reference materials by industry, product, solution area, and sales stage. At Adobe, the customer reference program produces one-page Customer Spotlights to promote big wins internally. Professional services consultants and deployment partners create Go-Live Briefs with detailed technical information, which Sales Engineers use as a technical sales tool.

Assign a single owner for all customer relationship programs, including references, customer advisory boards, and the customer briefing center. This enables program staff to get to know customers, understand why they endorse you, and which references are best suited for each situation. The program creates a single point of contact for sales reps, and eliminates redundant requests and over-use of marquee accounts.

Make references a standard part of the account management process. Add them into purchase contracts whenever possible. Require account managers to provide access to customers for post-sale interviews, and accept their guidance as to when and how to approach contacts. To cultivate a reference pipeline, track deal closures and "go-live" dates. Define a process for inviting customers into the program, presenting benefits, and creating content.

Use the reference program to provide value to customers. Give them opportunities to connect with peers from other companies, VIP passes to your conferences or to industry events, sneak peeks at upcoming products, or access to additional support or education. These benefits reward customers for their support and provide opportunities to interact that are not centered on selling or asking favors. Customers also benefit because the program team becomes their advocate and helps customers build stronger, more valuable relationships with your company.

Part IV
Context Defines Relevance and Value

Being relevant is like calling someone's name in a crowded room. People tune out all the surrounding noise to focus on their own conversation. Yet they tune in immediately when their own name is called. To get a response, you have to be loud enough to be heard over the din, of course. But if you simply add to the noise or call the wrong name, your target will not respond.

To "call the customer's name," understand what's valuable and useful in the customer's context. The following rules discuss how to achieve and demonstrate relevance in different stages of the customer lifecycle. They include ideas on creating a better discovery process, articulating and demonstrating tangible value, and developing messages and products that are relevant to individuals. The subsequent sections about solutions and industry specialization focus on two key paths to context-driven relevance.

20

Think Bottled Water, in a Desert

Understand what your customers' context dictates about value.

"An epicure, dining in Crewe
Once found a large mouse in his stew.
Said the waiter: "Don't shout, or wave it about
Or the rest will be wanting one, too.""

What's the real value of a bottle of water? Not much, if you're reading this book in a "developed country." In fact, if you take into account the toll on the environment from the manufacture, transport and disposal of all those plastic bottles, the value may well be negative. If you're among the one out of six people in the world without dependable safe drinking water, on the other hand, the value is significantly higher. Bottled water can keep you healthy and free from unpleasant diseases. At an extreme, it's the difference between life and death.

Context determines value. In three of the top four world consumers of bottled water—Brazil, Mexico, and China—the unreliability of safe tap water means that bottled water has demonstrable value. Americans, blessed as we are with treated, regulated tap water, purchase $15 billion worth of bottled water every year, a quarter of which is repackaged tap water. In the U.S., the value of bottled water is perceived, not demonstrable.

If you're selling to consumers, perception as value works. You may be able to position the mouse in the stew as a desirable and trend-setting feature. If you're selling to businesses, your offering had better be the equivalent of bottled water in a desert. Or at least, in a developing country. To sell big-ticket solutions to businesses that are mature enough to track metrics about their own business performance and the returns they receive on their investments, you need to be able to demonstrate measurable value.

Many businesses attempt to demonstrate value by creating a list of product features, then matching each to qualitative business benefits. Unless you've just invented a time machine, the problem with this approach is that most of your competitors have 80% of the same features. They can create the perception of the same benefits. To get beyond perception into demonstrating tangible value, there are two considerations.

Understand what your customers' context dictates about value. That context comes from external forces like industry and buyer trends, technology, competition, regulation, and changing social and/or economic environments. It also comes from characteristics of the customers themselves (see Rule 9). A great yet simple example of contextual value comes from business process automation. Systems that automate business processes provide significant savings because these tools reduce manual work and improve productivity. The ability to eliminate or better utilize hours of work by highly skilled staff translates into clear value that outweighs the cost of the software and implementation. Except in India. In India, where highly skilled staff work for a much smaller cost than their counterparts in North America and Europe, productivity may not be valuable enough to justify the cost of productivity-improving technology. The context requires a different set of value propositions.

Demonstrate value by showing specific changes in business metrics that you can impact. These changes are rarely the result of a specific product feature, but rather of the sum of all the features, perhaps in combination with other products and services (see Rule 25). Many companies make claims that their products help increase revenue, cut costs, and increase customer satisfaction. Of course, these are the mom-and-apple-pie of any business. Which is why everyone claims these benefits, and no one is believed. Get more specific about how you make a change to the quantitative and qualitative aspects of your customers' business environments. Rule 34 discusses how to create more tangible and believable value claims.

Know What It's For

Your impact on customers' business will be different for each use case.

Understanding a customer's industry and corporate objectives are the first steps in defining the context for your products. Unfortunately, many vendors stop there, with the result that the generic value propositions such as raising revenue, improving customer loyalty, and lowering cost lose credibility in the din.

A compelling value proposition must be relevant, as well as tangible, provable, and unique. Creating such value claims requires a deeper understanding of the use case—the purpose for which customers use your products or services. Use cases address the simple question of, "What's it for?" The answer is the key to identifying where and how you offer the greatest value. Consider, for example, a simple screw. It holds things together. But that general description fails to define its value. Holding a cabinet knob in place carries a very different value than holding together an airplane wing. The value depends on the use case much more than on the differences in materials or manufacturing.

Use cases consist of the scenarios, people, processes, and systems that contribute toward some corporate objective. Defining value within the context of a use case creates immediate relevance. Only through the use case can you fill in the details that lend credibility and demonstrate uniqueness in how your product's capabilities relate to high-level corporate objectives.

Find target use cases by identifying the business processes, functions, and challenges that most frequently form the context for customer purchases. Examine how critical each use case is to customers today and in the future, and what role you play within it. Use cases that are top of mind for customers and within which you can deliver significant benefits are those that warrant enhancements of products and services. Use cases where you can create significant impact, but which are lower priority for customers, can drive sales and marketing content, without changes to the product roadmap. Where your impact is smaller, consider participating in partners' solutions that target such use cases more directly.

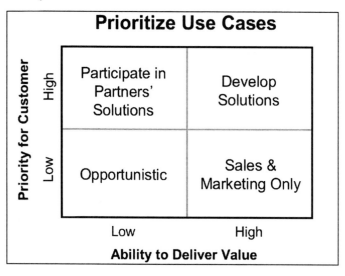

Figure 5: Selecting Target Use Cases

Interview customers to identify the key metrics within each use case, and how you've helped improve these. Learn the language decision makers use to describe their area of responsibility, and how they think about your products within that context. These testimonials create the basis of proof for use case-based value propositions.

To move away from a product-centric mentality, Informatica proactively engaged customers in developing use cases. The company hired a user experience team to help understand how customers worked with data, and how Informatica could help them. "The use case approach exposes what the customer is trying to get done, and therefore how they expect the solution to work," commented Judy Ko, SVP of Product Management and Marketing at Informatica. The approach has been so effective that use cases now drive Informatica's product roadmaps and cross-product requirements.

22 The Pudding Is in the Proof

Lay a path from your product to the customer's desired business results.

In school, just when we thought we had math all figured out, suddenly getting the right answer wasn't enough. Now you had to prove it and show your work. In business, showing customers the return on investment (ROI) is an extremely effective selling tool. In a 2009 survey of 120 B2B marketing and sales execs, industry-specific ROI analysis was ranked as the second most valuable sales tool, just behind case studies. Just like in school, however, the usefulness of an ROI does not come from the numbers. It comes from proving they are right.

There are three components to providing credible, tangible ROI: Existing customers willing to testify to the benefits they've received, a generalized model that explains how your product or service leads to business benefits, and the tools and expertise to apply that model to individual customer scenarios.

Whether in the form of a written case study, a simple quote, or a detailed analysis, customer testimony about quantitative improvements is indispensable to credibility. You can help ensure these testimonials support quantitative ROI claims in several ways. Understand which of the customer's metrics your products are likely to improve, and gather baseline information at the time of the sale. If even 10% of closed sales get such information, you'll have a valuable intelligence base. Return to customers after the product has been in use, and ask for data on the same metrics. Even customers unwilling to become public references will share data if they know it will be used anonymously and in aggregate. Build such data gathering into your customer reference program. Include quantitative metrics in the research done for every success story. Gathering metrics from existing customers will not only validate ROI claims, but also give individual sales reps great tools for repeat sales.

The second component of credible ROI is a generalized model. This is simply the detailed logical reasoning that lies behind your value proposition. To realistically show value, define a clear, logical path that connects the capabilities of your products or services to the customer's business objectives. Rule 23 describes the process for defining use case-driven value chains. After you've tested and validated the reasoning of your value chain with customers, use it as a consistent thread throughout your marketing material.

Finally, you will need to show the ROI for individual customer scenarios. This is especially important in accounts that require rigorous business cases in order to justify purchases. The paradox is that ROI tools that are sufficiently sophisticated to satisfy a detail-oriented financial buyer are often too complex for sales reps to use on their own. To develop detailed, customized business cases, you will need pre-sales resources or specialists involved in the budget justification stage of the sales cycle. The good news is that for many deals, a detailed ROI calculator is unnecessary. Teach reps to use and adapt ROI claims to specific customer situations by defining the logical path, or "value chain," from business results to product or solution capabilities. Even simple "back of the envelope" estimates of ROI can be sufficient once the customer has agreed with the logic of the value chain and with the assumptions.

Regardless of the specific tools, supplementing value claims with clear proof is critical. Lay a path from what you're selling to the customer's desired business results via the metrics that are relevant to the customer.

23 Build Logical Value Chains

A customer who agrees with your logic essentially agrees with your business case.

A key to creating a unique and credible value proposition is the ability to demonstrate why it's true in a way that is relevant to specific customer situations. The use case provides the basis for a direct, tangible, and quantifiable connection between what you offer and what the customer values. This use case-driven value chain defines the specifics of the relationships between products, tasks, processes, and objectives.

Develop value chains jointly with customers. Since the relationships within the value chain are the core of your business case, a customer who agrees with your logic essentially agrees with your business case before a single calculation is done.

To demonstrate the relationship between a product and high-level business objectives, build a use case-driven value chain from the top down, and from the bottom up. Determine how the use case relates to high-level business objectives. Next, drill down to the related objectives for the use case itself. There will be many objectives for any use case you identify. Build your business case around those that are of high importance to the customer, that you can influence, and that have quantitative measures or key business process indicators (KPIs) in place. Objectives that the customer is not measuring quantitatively are great components of the qualitative portion of your value proposition, but are insufficient to justify spending hard cash.

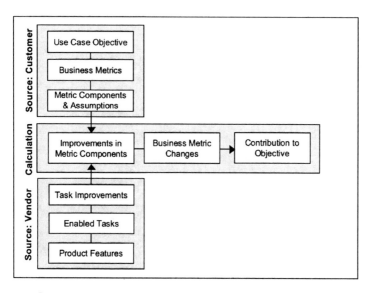

Figure 6: Building a Use Case-Driven Value Chain™

Each use case objective will have multiple processes and factors that contribute to its success. It's likely your customers track KPIs to measure these, or can estimate quantitatively some core metrics. In turn, each of these metrics is driven by more granular factors. Drill down to the elements that you can influence directly. While you identify what you can influence, note the metrics that you can't impact. They will be the assumptions within your business case.

From the bottom up, list the features and capabilities of your products. Identify which ones are relevant to the key tasks within the given use case. Look at past deployments, customer success stories, or conduct customer interviews to identify the quantitative improvements you've enabled in the performance of these key tasks.

Finally, connect the improvements in tasks to metrics you previously identified. Since you already know how these metrics relate to use case objectives, and how those objectives relate to corporate goals, you have a logical value chain in place. Before you plug in any numbers, it's absolutely critical to review this logical chain with your prospect and make sure they agree with the logic. If your current prospects agree that an agent's ability to take more calls and turn more cross-sell offers into sales is relevant to their contact center's objectives, your business case is built.

A workbook for defining Use Case-Driven Value™ is available at http://www.shirmangroup.com.

24 Compete on Experience

Assign an "audience experience manager."

Customer experience management (CEM) has been a popular concept for years. Though most of CEM's momentum is in the consumer marketing sphere, it is also very relevant for enterprise sales. Many companies have launched initiatives to "improve the online customer experience" or improve their sales process. Few have looked at their key audiences with an end-to-end perspective.

Different parts of your organization pay attention to different areas of customer interaction and behavior. Marketing tracks response to campaigns and the activities that result in the most qualified leads. Sales evaluates key turning points in the sales cycle. Support tracks common problem areas. You examine competitors from multiple perspectives. Product management does feature set comparisons and performance benchmarks. Marketing knows how competitors position themselves, where they show up in the Gartner Magic Quadrant or product award lists, and how their pricing and packaging works. Sales reps have silver bullets to highlight competitors' weaknesses. They know which competitors are strong in their accounts.

These are all indispensable components of business intelligence. Their common shortcoming is that they look at the customer and the market from your point of view, and not the customer's. Understanding and proactively managing the experiences of key audiences before, during, and after the sale can determine how quickly new customers move to make a purchase, and whether and when existing accounts will renew contracts. It will determine what they say to colleagues. That understanding is difficult to come by. A customer's experience with your company consists of scores of inter-actions: A visit to your booth at a conference. An email campaign executed by your internet marketing group. A blog post someone on a social networking site was promoting. The article they read in a magazine on a recent flight. The telemarketing call from your inside sales team. A conversation with a colleague. The sales meetings and demos that led to the sale. Contract negotiations. The professionalism and knowledge of your services team. The ease and usefulness of the product itself. The responsiveness of your support team.

Someone in your company has carefully considered each interaction individually—at least for those you control. Managing the experience of multiple audiences as they interact with many organizations and touch points requires a broad, cross-functional view. It requires proactive design of the impression that a string of experiences creates in total. Though a few companies have created customer advocates, these fre-quently focus only on relationships with the top existing accounts. To review, monitor and guide the end-to-end customer experience requires a broader charter.

Start by identifying your core audiences and the interactions you believe they are having with your company. Assign an "audience expe-rience manager" to each. This person or group will need visibility into the plans of multiple functional groups throughout the company. They will also need the power and influence to help align those plans and messages around a core set of customer experience objectives. The function requires competencies in brand-building, messaging, audience marketing, demand generation and sales process.

Some marketing departments have defined customer "personas" to help target their activities more precisely. The customer experience manager would go further, actually taking on the persona and interact-ing with the company the way that particular audience would, or hiring external analysts with no internal knowledge of the company to do so. The audience experience manager would build contacts and relation-ships among their target audience and keep close tabs on their reactions to specific interactions. Finally, they would work with diverse groups throughout the company to guide and adapt content and inter-actions to enhance and add consistency to customer experiences.

Even small tweaks in messaging can help create greater impact and better impressions. Five experiences that all point to the same, positive impressions are more valuable than ten that provide mixed messages. Evaluating end-to-end audience experiences also quickly uncovers internal disconnects, broken processes, and communication failures.

25 Separate Education and Sales

Customers know that sales reps are not trained or paid to provide objective, comprehensive education.

You don't pay or train your sales reps to provide objective, comprehensive education about your products. Yet, that is exactly what customers need early in the sales cycle, and what so many reps end up pretending to do. The result is an ill-informed customer who is distrustful of the information they received from your rep. *They know that your sales reps are not trained or paid to provide objective, comprehensive education.*

This is a big issue if you are selling a significantly new product. One example is social networking technology. Adoption among adult consumers has quadrupled in just three years, with over half of 25- to 34-year-olds, and one-third of 35- to 45-year-olds now participating. Only a small number, however, use social networking internally within their companies. Scores of start-ups are trying to educate enterprises about how social networking and other "2.0" applications are relevant to their business. Because customers lack experience with social media within the enterprise, vendors must spend precious sales-cycle time and expensive sales resources to educate prospects. This is wasteful for the vendors. It is also inadequate for customers, who have difficulty separating salesmanship from the realistic benefits of a new technology. *They know the sales reps are not trained or paid to provide objective, comprehensive education.*

If you are selling to a relatively mature market, this is still an issue. Buyers in mature markets are more informed and have hands-on experience with the product or its competitors. They tend to scrutinize any information about new products and features more closely. Unless customers find an unbiased source of information before they ever encounter your sales rep, they will have to get educated by your sales rep, whom they won't entirely trust. Because *they know that your sales reps*...you get the idea.

There are several alternatives for educating outside the sales cycle. Which you select hinges on your willingness to increase transparency. Customers are the best third-party source of objective information. Provide forums where prospects can connect with each other and with existing customers. Such forums can exist online in user communities, and offline at industry conferences. Provide ways for the participants to access accurate information about your company and products. Partners and industry pundits are also great objective, trustworthy sources. Make sure they too have access to accurate information and to each other, and are available to customers.

The internet provides some fantastic forums to which customers turn to gather unbiased product and vendor information. Unfortunately, it's difficult to distinguish accurate information from rumors, hearsay, and mistakes. To help keep information accurate, find out what online information sources your customers use, and what's being said there about your company and products. Participate regularly in the conversation. Have product management, not sales or marketing, answer questions about features. Encourage and provide time for professional services and support people to weigh in on questions. Identify the most active members of the forum, and provide them with up-to-date documentation and information—not marketing collateral! Rather than seeking to control these third-party interactions, you can leverage them as education vehicles simply by enabling them and participating in the discussion. That means not only talking, but listening (see Rules 15 and 17 on soliciting customer ideas).

Shift education away, and ahead of, the sales cycle. Your expensive direct sales resources will save time. Your sales cycles will get shorter. A better-informed market will be more confident in information about you because they receive objective, comprehensive education.

R u l e

26

Use Services Strategically

Ongoing involvement by the service organization can turn account management into a truly continuous and value-generating process.

Interviews with the customers of one highly successful technology company provided a clear example of how services can enhance ongoing customer relevance. Though the customers were all extremely happy with the results they had achieved, we asked if there was anything else the company could do to further increase the value of its products. A majority of the accounts said they wished the vendor would come back periodically to make sure customers were getting the most out of their purchase.

That's more than a services revenue opportunity. It's the chance to strengthen customer relationships and show your commitment to your customer's success. Your, or your partner's, services organization is a great place to execute on that commitment. It's likely you have service, support, and education offerings. It's also likely they are reactive. If service and support is not sold with the product, contact with the customer may only happen if or when there is a problem. To demonstrate and deliver on your promises of value, create services that are proactive in nature.

BEA Systems used proactive services to solidify key customer relationships. The company was seeing a decline in renewals of enterprise license agreements, despite growth in the overall market. The feedback the company got from customers was to "get ingrained in our initiatives and understand our business." You fly in once a year when it's time to renew the contract, and never check in in-between to see how my previous deployments are going."

In response, BEA launched an innovative program that would put BEA experts at the heart of their best customers' IT organizations. The company created Global Service Executives, who were responsible for all services across education, consulting, and support. A portion of their compensation was based on the customers' ongoing success and full utilization of all purchased products. In addition, a Client Architect was placed on-site with strategic accounts, reporting to the customer's CIO. These new sales team members were in position to see customers' real needs from the inside, and to participate in helping customers create strategy and roadmaps. The result was a shift from simple implementation services to more consultative ones, and increased use of pre-sales consulting and training programs. The resulting services-led sales produced larger product deals.

Use proactive services to create an account management approach that covers the entire customer lifecycle. Though a program like BEA's can be expensive, many companies incorporate similar resources into the top support tiers. Other options are to offer more pre-sales assessments that ensure the customer fully understands requirements and how a new solution will fit within their existing business. Periodic post-sale audits that assess progress toward specific business objectives set at the time of purchase are another great way to ensure customer success. You can also create broader programs that leverage intelligence from your support and services organization to create ongoing value for customers. Produce and publish summaries of lessons learned from similar deployments, or from certain categories of support calls. These contribute much more to customers' success, and to their future business with you, than the typical marketing mailing customers are receiving now.

By de-emphasizing the license sale as the focal point, ongoing involvement by the service organization can turn account management into a truly continuous and value-generating process that drives both service and technology sales. Customers that buy services buy more technology products because they are more successful and more satisfied with past purchases, and because they perceive less risk in adopting new technology.

Part V
Succeeding with Solutions

The development of complete solutions can combat commoditization, raise average deal size, and engage more senior decision makers. Unfortunately, solution creation efforts often stall due to internal disagreements about what the solutions are, and how much to invest in creating them. B2B vendors have options about how they go to market with solutions and the role they play in a complete solution stack. The following rules are a guide to help you move from mere marketing spiel to the creation of solutions that provide greater value for customers and revenue growth for your company.

27 Solution Selling May Suffice

Solution selling does not create new value. It communicates the value you already offer.

Almost every management team that has contemplated offering solutions has had that very long discussion about "what exactly is a solution?" Sixty-six minutes later, people look exasperated and have made no decisions. What's clear is that you must link your offerings more closely with customers' business needs. Unfortunately, the team disagrees on what solutions are and how much the company should invest in developing them.

You might not need to build and sell solutions. You may just need to learn "solution selling." The term "solution selling" has been overused and misused, so let's define it. Products, product sales and marketing, solution selling and marketing, and solutions lie along a spectrum of "solutionliness." That's a horrible word, and I promise never to use it again. It does convey the right sense of a continuum. On one end are products, which supply specific functionality to perform a particular task. Product selling is about features and functions. On the other end are full-fledged solutions (see Rule 26) that address a complete business need.

Solution selling is in the middle of our continuum of solutionliness. (Okay, I lied. But this really is the last time.) Solution selling places products or services in the context of customers' needs and goals. Products are evaluated on the basis of how they contribute to those goals, in addition to how they compare functionally. Solution selling does not require that you provide a complete solution; only that you understand the role your products or services play within one. While solution selling communicates value more effectively and accurately and results in a more constructive sales process, don't delude yourself or your sales channel into thinking that the same products become more valuable if they are sold differently.

Solution selling is first and foremost about entering your customers' context. It requires an understanding of what is compelling the purchase. Chances are, your customer didn't decide they need your product for the bragging rights of owning it. A specific person in a specific role, being evaluated against specific metrics, decided they need to accomplish some objective. They are considering many different ways to reach their goals. To enter that context, your sales reps will need to understand how the product will be used, and what business processes, metrics, and objectives the customer wants to affect with the purchase.

To help sales succeed at solution selling, invest in sales education (Rule 39), and in solution marketing. Only then can you generate the right types of leads, set the stage for appropriate sales conversations, and supply the education and tools that reps will need to move opportunities through the entire sales cycle. Solution marketing differs from product marketing in several ways:

- Solutions marketers understand what motivates customers to allocate budget within the broader context for a purchase.
- Solutions marketing content is focused on the buyer and their objectives, not the product or its features.
- Solutions-oriented value propositions focus on specific use cases or situations in which the customer is involved.
- The solutions marketing process and programs provide information or resources that are valuable to the customer.
- Thought leadership and value creation are critical components of solutions marketing.
- Solutions marketing activity often involves collaboration with other companies (see broader context in the first bullet).
- To ensure that all of the above are truly relevant and evolve with the customer, Solutions Marketing must engage the customer in conversation and dialogue.

You'll also need service offerings—whether internal or through partners —that help integrate the purchase into the broader customer initiative it was meant to support. Though solution selling requires less investment than developing solutions, alignment of your organization around the customer needs that are the focus of solution selling will help you deliver on the impact you promised.

28 Mousetraps Don't Eliminate Rodent Infestations

A solution is a proven, integrated combination of products, services, and expertise, and requires changes in customer behavior.

In their enthusiasm to show value to customers, marketers often use the words "solution" and "product" interchangeably. This obscures a very real distinction. A product addresses a specific requirement, or the need to perform a particular task: Automate a business process, personalize online campaigns, communicate with mobile employees. A solution, on the other hand, addresses the driver or strategic imperative that causes the customer to allocate budget. Such drivers are often strategic imperatives such as improving customer retention through more differentiated and intimate relationships, or scaling to handle a higher volume of business while maintaining service levels and controlling cost.

To illustrate the difference between products and solutions, let's use mice. Not computer mice. Live mice. Let's say you walk into the kitchen for your 1:00 am snack, and as you stare indecisively into the open refrigerator, you notice the shuffling of tiny feet along the wall and glimpse a quick-moving shadow as the invader scrambles behind the dishwasher. "Mousetrap!" you say to yourself, and make plans to purchase one the next morning. Placing mousetraps in every corner and sprinkling poison behind the refrigerator will probably kill the mouse. Unfortunately, it will not keep new ones from showing up. You need a solution, not just a couple of products.

Permanently eliminating rodent infestations may require a visit by a pest control service. To prevent future invasions, you may need to adopt a cat, sprinkle cat-safe mouse repellent around the house, change the way you dispose of garbage, and adopt more stringent cleaning habits. You may need to hire a cleaning service. It will be ideal if a trusted friend shares with you their proven methods and recommendations for their favorite pest control or cleaning service.

The solution is not one product or even a combination of products. It is a proven, integrated combination of products, services, and expertise. Most importantly, its success depends on a different set of factors. A product is considered successful if it contains a rich features set, performs reliably, can be put into use quickly, and is simple and inexpensive to maintain. A solution, on the other hand, requires some level of integration among its components. The roles of the various parties that come together to provide a solution must be clearly delineated. A solution must be able to evolve to the customer's evolving needs. Most importantly, the success of a solution requires real commitment to substantial changes in customer behavior.

Because products and solutions differ in the scope of the problems they address and components they provide, the resources and skillsets required to sell them successfully are also widely different. Moving from a product focus to the development and sales of solutions requires significant financial investment, and the cultivation of new skillsets within the organization. Such investment can be spread out over time. Reference and then solution selling can develop the required skills and assets to lay the groundwork for a full solution offering in the long term.

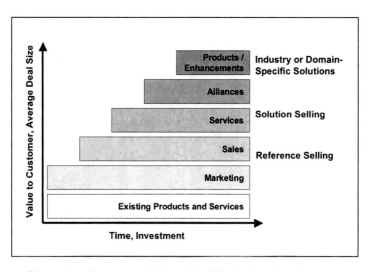

Figure 7: Degree and Breadth of Solution Development

29 The Orchestra Has Many Instruments

Solution delivery invariably involves inter-company collaboration.

To realistically assess the required investment and likely returns of offering a solution, companies must first understand what role they will play in a solution stack. That will determine key decisions, including product development investment, required sales capabilities, and alliance strategy. There are four types of participants in a complete solution:

- **Orchestrators** provide the thought leadership and define the solution. They own the intellectual property to a substantial portion of the functionality or capabilities that address customers' needs.

- **Completers** offer niche products with a narrow scope of functionality that is critical to the success of the overall solution. Completers solidify their role in a solution stack by clearly defining the value they provide to the orchestrator and to the end-customer. Their goal is to participate in every sale the orchestrator makes. They do so by simplifying the adoption and use of their product or service alongside the orchestrator's offering, or completely embedding their functionality through OEM agreements.

- **Complementors** provide products or services that enhance the effectiveness, efficiency, or attractiveness of the solution, but are not critical. Complementors have a tougher sell than Completers, as their offerings lie on the periphery of the solution. Orchestrators will concede to customer choice of complementary vendors. That means Complementors can expect to encounter competitors' products as alternatives within the same solution. Complementors must enhance both their product and the customers' mindset to transform their core offering into an essential part of the solution. In other words, they must transform themselves (or the customers' perception of them) into completers.

- **Delivery Experts** are the companies who make the solution usable and easier to adopt for the end-customers. In construction, they are the general contractors. In event marketing, the event management companies play this role. Delivery experts have relationships with all solution participants and the experience to know how best to assemble them into the best possible solution. Not surprisingly, delivery experts and orchestrators are often the same company.

In enterprise software, the role of orchestration was traditionally held by System Integrators. In recent years, the larger vendors have taken on the task, not coincidentally expanding their own consulting capabilities. These vendors have recognized that developing an ecosystem of completing and complementary technologies makes their products more attractive for SIs to adapt and recommend. IBM, Oracle, and many others offer industry and use case-specific solutions based on their completely horizontal (e.g. industry-neutral) software. To create the solutions, they partner with other software vendors for key capabilities such as content management, application performance management, and analytics. Over time, they acquire completing offerings to be able to offer more of the solution footprint on their own. As orchestrators of the solution, the platform vendors also assemble ecosystems of complementary technologies that include industry-specific applications such as billing for telecommunications or risk management for financial services. Finally, they rely on both internal resources and third-party SIs to play the role of delivery expert. Though the SIs have hardly given up their role in assembling solutions, they are also attracted by the solutions created by others. Their complexity and breadth present vast services revenue opportunities.

Until a vendor formally creates and begins to sell a solution, the customer orchestrates the solutions they need for their business. They collect and assemble the needed components and develop expertise internally or via consultants. By taking over the work and complexity, the orchestrator creates significant value for the customer that reaches far beyond the vendor's own products.

It is common for a single company to play more than one role. Even so, solution delivery invariably involves inter-company collaboration. From the customer's point of view, a successful solution will be one where the collaboration is so well-planned that the boundaries between the participants are invisible.

30 You Don't Have to Be the Conductor

Orchestration is the most desired role, but also the most risky.

For the majority of companies, taking on the role of solution orchestrator is the most tempting. Orchestrators exercise the greatest control over the evolution of a solution. They take on a strategic role in the eyes of the end-customer and create closer relationships with top decision makers than do completers or complementors. To orchestrate solutions successfully, however, requires significant investment and a broad set of competencies. Selecting the wrong solution or underestimating the effort required to bring it to market can waste resources and undermine revenue growth. The combination of investment requirements and uncertainty make orchestration the most risky role.

A different role in the solution stack may be a better option if your company lacks the resources to build the solution and lead the go-to-market efforts. Another reason to forego the lead role is if your products or services make up a relatively small part of a larger purchase. That is, the value you can bring to customers in a particular solution area is relatively small. If the customer's buying process centers on another category of product, you will need to determine how your offering relates to the one that is central in the customer's view. Once you understand the role your product plays within the broader solution from your customer's point of view, you're ready to pursue partnerships that will allow you to profit from the opportunity.

Providers of content and applications for next-generation communications services are taking on completer and complementor roles with great success. Communication services providers (CSPs) are orchestrating packages of voice, data, and entertainment services to create solutions that meet the needs of many diverse customer segments. Such solutions may include core network infrastructure and applications from the primary CSP, bandwidth leased from other CSPs, devices such as mobile phones, routers, and set top boxes from electronics manufacturers, and third-party content and applications such as ring tones, stock quotes and news feeds, or teleconferencing software. The need for a constant stream of innovative services creates an opportunity for companies that otherwise would never have been able to gain a foothold in the highly complex, consolidated and capital-intensive communications industry.

The success of complementary products lies in the ability to create and manage strong partnerships. As with any partnership, determine where your product fits within the bigger picture, and be ready to articulate how your products or services enhance the value of the overall solution. The company orchestrating the solution is likely to have critical gaps in their own offerings. They are also looking to fill these, and to recruit "nice to have" complementary product and service providers. The orchestrator is building an ecosystem. Your job is to optimize your position within it in order to maximize market reach, revenue, and profit.

You will need to share responsibility for integrating, selling, and supporting your product with the orchestrating vendor. Establish whether brand recognition is important to you for continued growth in this market. If so, you will need the partner to acknowledge that they've incorporated your product into their own. Select partners whose product are compatible and easy to integrate with, in order to avoid investments in design and development that cannot be re-used for other relationships. If your product provides a key capability that completes the orchestrator's solution, you are likely to get less visibility, but also carry less responsibility for integration, support, and sales.

Competition for the most complete feature set often turns complementary products into completers. In the communications market, functions such as digital video recorders and mobile location-based services are currently considered nice-to-have complementary features. There is no doubt that just like voice mail or text messaging, such capabilities will soon become must-haves. The complementors that supply them today will stand to benefit significantly as their role evolves to completer.

Ecosystems Power Solutions

Ecosystems create market momentum and erect formidable barriers for competitors.

The entertainment industry knows how to take a single product and turn it into a galaxy of merchandise. If you have kids, you know that a movie may be the beginning of a year-long obsession with toys, clothing, bedding, school supplies, books, and who-knows-what-else. In the B2B realm, many vendors sell education, support, or professional services that complement their products, but stop short of building a complete ecosystem. That requires recruiting complementary vendors to offer products and services that expand the value and usefulness of your own offerings. Ecosystems create market momentum and erect formidable barriers for competitors.

One great example is Microsoft Windows' victory over the Apple Macintosh. In the 1990's, Microsoft beat out the better-designed Apple operating system through the creation of an enormous and well-supported ecosystem of third-party application vendors.

Apple started as a product-focused company; and almost disappeared, despite its loyal following among educators and designers. Its computers were easier to use and better designed. But the mass market of buyers who needed easy-to-use computers was only beginning to appear. For them, computers still held only limited usefulness.

While Apple concentrated on great product design, Microsoft opened the interfaces to its product and wooed a broad community of software developers to meet the growing demand for specialized applications. Microsoft understood that an army of software companies would generate greater momentum and demand for their operating system than Apple could ever do alone. The path to securing the market was an ecosystem, and Apple missed that opportunity completely in its early years.

Apple has learned from past mistakes. When music sharing emerged, launching wars between record labels and music enthusiasts, Apple recognized a new need, and designed around it. This time, Apple focused on the customer in addition to the design, with savvy marketing and even savvier ecosystem creation. Apple has created an ecosystem of music licensing companies, toy-makers, car-makers, and even furniture and clothing manufacturers for its consumer-oriented iPod line. It's questionable whether those horrible iPod-enabled lima-bean shaped "chairs" ever helped sell an iPod, but the ecosystem of complementary products has created an entry barrier that is almost impossible to surmount, and has established Apple as the premier player in a completely re-made music industry. As this book is being written, Apple is repeating that strategy with the iPhone, touting tens of thousands of new third-party applications.

You can take the first step towards an ecosystem before ever entering a new market, creating a product, or designing a solution. Determine whether the new market or offering is likely to generate demand for complementary products and services that will increase its overall value to the customer. Then, identify which kinds of partners could be involved in offering related products. Design and package your product or service to simplify the addition of third-party products. Consider also how you'll claim the ecosystem as your own. This can range from something as a simple as a compatibility logo to co-branded marketing tools and products.

Finally, recruit the required alliances to form the core of your ecosystem, starting with completers and implementers, and finally complementors. As with any effective alliance, explicitly define each partner's expectations from and contributions to the solution. Agree on ownership of the intellectual property surrounding product integration and responsibilities for various levels of customer support. Ensure that you have clear rules of engagement for sales opportunities and that both sales organizations are aware of them.

32

Get Ready, Set, Juggle!

Ignoring any one area could prevent the solution from reaching its full potential.

Companies often underestimate the investment and challenges of launching solution offerings. Initially, some view a solution as simply a different marketing approach to existing products. While this may get some traction at first, customers quickly recognize that there are missing pieces and that the company is over-promising on results. A vendor who markets a solution while still offering a product will find that previously satisfied customers turn to larger, more horizontally-integrated vendors to meet raised expectations.

To deliver a complete solution, be ready to balance many internal requirements. Complement marketing efforts with investment in sales skills, new alliances, and product enhancements or integration. Ignoring any one area could prevent the solution from reaching its full potential for revenue and account penetration, and lead to customer defections.

- Select the use cases where the solution can provide the greatest value, and which customers see as critical to their success. (See Rule 21 for more on use cases.)

- Identify all the audiences who influence solution purchases. They are likely to be different from the people who made decisions about individual product purchases. For each decision maker, pinpoint the objectives that will be positively influenced. (See Rules 15, 17, and 18.)

- Determine what functionality is critical, and how to make the solution most readily usable by customers. For the initial phase, zero in on the core solution components. At the same time, begin to develop a roadmap for the capabilities and partners that you will want to add as the solution evolves. (See Rule 28 for a model of how solutions evolve.)

- Gain agreement from and/or educate all key solution participants—marketing, sales, support, services, and partners—on the contribution they will be making to selling and delivering solutions. (See Rules 3 and 4 about cross-functional execution.)

- Assess the capabilities and skills of your sales reps and channel partners. You'll need to invest in education and tools to enhance existing skills. To drive early sales and continue the transfer of skills and expertise to the sales force, deploy specialists with in-depth solution and domain expertise. Specialists must have two objectives: help close solution deals, and educate sales reps to be capable of selling the solution independently. (See Rules 37 through 41 on channel empowerment.)

- Articulate concrete value of the complete solution, and back it up with deployed customer success stories. Talk to customers about the measurable impact they seek from a complete solution, and closely track the business impact of pilots and early deployments. Test your reasoning about benefit and ROI claims with customers to ensure it's credible. (See Rules 19 through 23 about discovering and proving value.)

- Go to market in phases to balance investment and return. Begin with a well-defined, small group of accounts, and expand after a minimal number of these have been sold and deployed. Rushing to a broad market too quickly, and without adequate references, experience, and processes in place can frustrate both your sales organization and customers. (See Rule 36 on stages of industry specialization, which are similar for horizontal solutions as well.)

- Expect a learning curve and actively manage the solution's evolution. (See Rule 6 about uncertainty.)

Assembling or participating in a solution can elevate a company's visibility within target accounts and raise average sales prices. Solutions gain the attention of new, often more powerful, decision makers. By focusing the discussion on value, solutions command higher average sale price, and raise average deal size. Because they cultivate an ecosystem of partners, solutions turn that ecosystem into a virtual expanded sales force. Most importantly, solutions give companies the opportunity to address the buyer's most essential needs, transforming their relationship with customers from tactical product vendor to trusted problem-solver.

Part VI
Live In Your Customer's Universe

The previous sections described methods to become better connected and more relevant to customers. To fully grasp and address your customers' needs, it's essential to comprehend the markets within which they operate. Their industry, not yours, is the universe within which customers' priorities, challenges, and objectives exist. The rules in this section help provide that perspective.

Many of the recommendations in this section are based on studies conducted by The Shirman Group in 2008 and 2009[x] on industry specialization by companies selling products and services to other companies, and on work done directly with vendors pursuing vertical markets. The findings from both surveys and in-depth interviews reveal that specialization of marketing, sales, services, products, and partnerships around key target industries produces significant improvements in revenue and brand awareness within those industries.

33 If You're Horizontal, Stand Up

Specializing around vertical markets presents an enormous opportunity for growth.

Many B2B vendors offer products or services that are useful in multiple industries and usage situations. An enormous opportunity for growth lies in the fact that the same capabilities play a very different role at companies in different industries. Depending on the vertical markets they participate in, customers may see what you provide as mission-critical, or "nice to have"—at the core of a revenue stream, or part of a cost center. Customers in different industries also use different languages to describe their businesses and their needs. Do your customers earn their revenue from customers, clients, subscribers, or accounts? When they fulfill orders, do they ship, activate provision, approve memberships, or open accounts? When they bill, is consolidation, mediation, collection, rights management, or risk management their main concern?

Specializing around vertical markets presents an enormous opportunity for growth for companies selling to enterprise customers. In our 2009 study of industry specialization by B2B companies, over 70% reported that industry specialization had a positive impact on revenue. Two-thirds planned to further increase the level of specialization in key vertical markets. Companies that have focused on target verticals have improved customer relationships, increased competitiveness, identified more sales opportunities, engaged more senior buyers, and accelerated revenue growth.[xi] Demonstrate that you understand their world, and you can serve customers better and close more business. So get vertical!

Despite the benefits that industry specialization provides, I've come across multiple companies where some portion of the executive team strongly resists any industry-specific investment. The common concerns are that industry specialization will turn the company into a niche player, fragment sales and product development efforts, or damage the company's position as the underlying platform for an entire ecosystem. These concerns represent an all-or-nothing view. Re-organizing the entire company along industry lines is usually not the end goal. Aligning key sales, marketing, service, and development resources to key customer segments makes the organization more customer-centric. In fact, industry alignment can begin small, and expand only as fast and as far as is appropriate for your company.

You may consider a vertical focus in reaction to requests from existing accounts, or to protect market share from competitors. In other cases, there may be the opportunity to prevent commoditization or proactively drive growth. The following situations are good indicators that you should consider some level of industry specialization.

Reactive indicators:
- Customers expect expertise, proof points, product content, or services that are specific to their industry.
- You are losing deals to competitors who have closer relationships with the customer.
- Your product is losing its differentiation as competitors catch up on features and value.
- Your sales reps have difficulty in justifying price, and deals fail in the budgeting phase.
- Your horizontal product lags behind the market leaders, but appeals to niche markets, and can be adapted to dominate those niches.

Proactive indicators:
- An industry's spend in your market space is growing faster than your company's revenue is growing in that industry.
- You want to penetrate further into existing accounts or increase average deal size.
- You want to engage high-level decision makers concerned with business rather than technical or functional issues.
- Your company's growth is creating a critical mass of resources within marketing, sales and services to allow for greater specialization and improved customer focus in key markets.

What if your company is already the leader in a horizontal market and has the strongest offering for solving a specific problem? In this situation, your primary focus will be on consolidating the market and dominating horizontally. Even then, paying attention to industry-specific customer needs can enhance sales and marketing efforts.

34 Select Target Verticals with Care

Return on investment will depend on two factors: the size of the opportunity, and your company's ability to pursue it.

Specialization implies prioritization and the decisions of whether and how much to invest in each target vertical market. The return on investment will depend on two factors: the size of the opportunity, and your company's ability to pursue it successfully. Use the opportunity and execution factors listed in Rule 4.

To find the largest opportunities, look at industries where you have significant traction due to historically high demand, and those that are likely to grow in the future. Symantec Corp., a leading vendor of information security and storage products, created industry marketing teams for financial services, communications, and government—all historically strong sectors. In addition, Symantec selected the healthcare industry, because forecasts showed enormous future growth there. Healthcare companies were going paperless just as privacy regulations were enacted and data theft skyrocketed: the perfect storm for data management and security demand. By looking outside their traditional strongholds, Symantec was able to benefit from the rapid growth in a new market.

The framework in Figure 8 summarizes strategies for different types of industries, and the subsequent step (described in Rule 21) of prioritizing use cases.

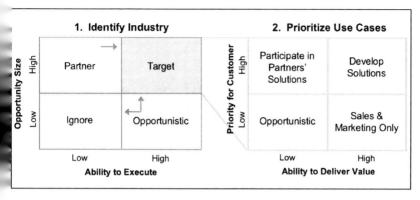

Figure 8: Selecting Target Industries and Use Cases

Ignore (small opportunity, low ability to execute): Ignore vertical markets with low expenditures on the types of products or services you offer. If companies in this industry are on your managed account list, consider replacing them with ones in more promising verticals. Move these off to the channel or inside sales.

Opportunistic (small opportunity, strong ability to execute): These industries spend little compared to other markets and are not demonstrating promise of future growth. For historical reasons, you have a dominant position and expertise. Keep investment down to maintenance levels. Do not add any industry-specific resources, but allow sales reps with productive accounts to continue to pursue. Look for changes that may suggest increasing investment or conversely re-deploying sales resources to more promising accounts.

Partner (big opportunity, limited ability to execute): Where the opportunity is significant but you lack a reference base, appropriate feature set, domain expertise, or other key capabilities, identify partners interested in orchestrating a solution and position yourself as a key completer, or at least as a complementor. Over time, you may gain the capabilities and critical mass to pursue these industries more aggressively.

Target (big opportunity, strong ability to execute): Industries with high spend and/or growth and where you are positioned to execute should be the primary targets for investment. Hire additional expertise, invest in press and analyst relations, and promote past successes. Within target industries, evaluate individual use cases or solution areas to determine the extent and direction of sales, marketing, alliance, and engineering specialization. (See Rule 21 for more on use cases.)

35 Industry Specialization Can Start Small

The support of industry specialists is critical to early sales rep success.

Close behind the question of "Which industries?" follows "how many?" Industry specialization can be implemented in phases, and offers rewards even for small, focused levels of investment.

When IBM first made the decision to specialize, the industry solutions team developed a business case based on a detailed analysis of customers' purchase decision processes. The analysis showed that industry solutions would accelerate the sales process and enlarge deals. Increased services revenue—both for IBM and its business partners—was also a key part of the business case. The long-term plan included industry solution support from every function, from a sales re-organization, to demand generation, branding, event participation, product development, and channel and partner management. In the short term, however, only a few key changes in sales and marketing were put in place. A highly focused pilot addressed just a few top industries, and only within specific geographies. IBM identified a handful of accounts as initial targets, with the goal of winning just two or three. These companies were the marquee names in each industry, and would create credibility for any broader initiatives in those sectors.

IBM made some key organizational and operational changes from the beginning. They created a VP-level lead for each target industry. A quick inventory of sales skills in the pilot regions identified reps who were already specialized by virtue of having a high concentration of target industry accounts. (Meanwhile reps who had five or more industries on their existing account lists were immediately disqualified as not having sufficient industry depth.) The small sales teams reported to the industry VPs, and carried industry-only quotas. In addition, IBM created a sales overlay organization to provide yet another level of industry and solution expertise. Finally, IBM implemented a completely new set of industry codes to ensure that the company could identify and track revenue by industry. This made accurate and consistent metrics possible.

Three key success factors to launching pilot industry specialization efforts:

Laser focus on a few key accounts. Select these accounts only after developing a good understanding of the competitive dynamics within the target industry. That's because some companies may refuse to do the same thing as their competitors—no matter how successful the latter may be. Bank of America and Wells Fargo are examples of such "if they do it, we won't" attitudes. In telecommunications, cable providers would never consider a satellite company as a credible example, but will look to other communication service providers. Customers won't tell you that your big brand-name reference lacks all credibility inside their organization. The only way to know is to ask an industry insider.

High-level ownership and clear, measurable revenue goals. "Success in the industry only comes when senior management actively believes in this as an agenda. Someone has to own the number," suggested David Miner, VP of Industry Marketing at Symantec. If no one owns "the number" for an industry, no amount of marketing effort will get you there. Hand-in-hand with setting specific objectives, of course, is the ability to accurately measure results. Don't let the complexity of changing your sales operation system derail you. I've seen industry groups in a $5 billion+ company use manual processes to extract industry revenue data. That's not a long-term solution, of course, and hardly a best practice. It does show that bad data can be overcome to ensure everyone knows exactly how much impact industry specialization is having.

Support sales with industry specialists. Unless you acquire a company and a sales channel that is already specialized in an industry, the support of specialists is critical to early sales rep success. The first wins will be key for building external credibility and generating internal momentum. Your ability to build a business case for expanding industry specialization efforts and recruiting additional sales resources will depend on the success of the pilot deals.

36 Define Your Specialization Roadmap

To advance beyond the reactive stage, the single most important factor is executive sponsorship.

The appropriate amount and depth of industry focus varies from company to company, and over time. Like any other part of your business, industry alignment requires processes for planning and frameworks for decision-making. Create a roadmap for your industry-specific capabilities that includes criteria for industry selection, metrics and milestones to measure progress, and guidelines for evaluating subsequent investments. Use industry business plans to guide execution and communicate action plans to internal organizations and partners.

The spectrum of maturity in industry specialization begins with reactive tactics in response to individual opportunities. Such isolated activities are often "skunk-works" rather than corporate initiatives. To become more proactive, the single most important factor is executive sponsorship. Prepare a business case that demonstrates the expected impact of specialization on net new sales. Our studies show that even in the first two years of implementing industry-focused activity, 40% of companies see notable or significant increases in revenue. After three years, 70% see revenue growth, and after five years, almost 80% do.

Once there is adequate support for investment in vertical markets, focus on three or fewer industries. Recruit personnel with industry-specific expertise. Establish processes for planning, pursuing, and measuring industry growth. At this stage, IT changes are unlikely to get funding, so find alternative ways to baseline and track revenue in target verticals. For companies with horizontal products, Sales and Marketing organizations should be actively engaged in industry efforts, and Services, Channels, and Alliances should at least be aware of likely upcoming changes in customer expectations and partner relationships.

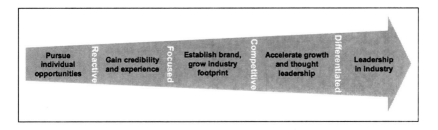

Figure 9:   Evolution of Industry Specialization

Companies that are competitive in their industry efforts have this go-to-market strategy as an executive priority. Be sure this management foundation exists. Additional investments in vertical markets will be largely wasted without it. Reaching a competitive level requires that you enlist participation from all relevant organizations and commitment from key partners. Consistently measure the effectiveness of industry strategy, and conduct regular executive reviews. At this stage, you are likely to re-organize parts of the sales organization, build industry-specific product enhancements, and assemble or participate in cross-vendor industry solutions.

The stage of greatest maturity for industry alignment is clear differentiation and market leadership within one or more target verticals. At this stage, industries are managed as lines of business, with executive responsibility for industry P&L. You need not re-organize the company around vertical markets, but do manage verticals as businesses alongside non-industry-aligned divisions. To reach this level, contribute industry thought leadership and establish strong relationships with industry partners, analysts, and press. Invest in processes and systems to enable industry-specific operations.

For many companies, a focused effort in marketing, sales, and services targeted at a few industries drives significant growth. You don't need to reach the most advanced stage of industry specialization. By proactively aligning even parts of your business to your customers', you can become more relevant and deliver greater value to key markets.

Part VII
Nurture Your Channels

Relevance starts with products. It continues with marketing messages. But the place where your company's ability to engage and convince customers of value culminates is in the sales channel. Countless strategies and initiatives fail because sales channel acceptance or capability are lacking. Your company's agility to try new initiatives and pursue new opportunities depends on the ability of your sales channels to adapt. Use the following rules to empower direct sales forces and indirect channels with the skills to articulate relevance and execute on growth strategies.

37 Eliminate the Sales-Marketing Divide

Start thinking about Sales as your customer.

Do your marketing and sales organizations work as one seamless team to promote your company and sell your products? Unfortunately, the vast majority of medium and large companies will answer "no," or "only sometimes," to these questions. Both sales and marketing organizations recognize the challenge. According to a CSO Insights survey[xii] of top sales effectiveness initiatives for 2009, "more closely aligning sales and marketing" was among the top three priorities. Red Herring's survey of CMOs[xiii] also showed that marketing and sales alignment is a top strategic issue, with 42% of the respondents giving it a nine or ten (highest ranking) as a crucial issue to address.

Some complaints often heard from sales and marketing people are indicative of the common tension: "I don't have time to read all the stuff marketing puts out, it's too difficult to find, and most of it is useless anyway." "Sales can't see beyond quarter end." "Marketing is more worried about the colors in the presentation than the real issues I face when I meet with customers." "Sales just doesn't get this new way of selling. We need to hire different sales people."

"Start thinking about Sales as your customer," recommends Rick Jackson, CMO at VMWare. "If you just focus on the end customer, not on what the channel has to do to engage them, then you're not serving your real audience," he adds.

Rick recalls that when joined BEA Systems to head its product marketing function, he found an organization that was uncoordinated internally, and disconnected from Sales. Marketing had been so enamored with evangelizing the technology that they had not made the effort to understand how the product was actually bought and sold. During his first two weeks at BEA, Rick talked to sales people. He asked what tools and content they were using, what they got from Marketing or created themselves. His objective was to understand how they got their job done, and how Marketing could help. With the under-standing of how Sales really pursued opportunities and closed deals, Rick re-aligned Product Marketing to enable and accelerate that process.

The lessons from BEA and other companies who have addressed this issue head on are clear. One is that Marketing has to know how to sell the product. Understand the sales process, and what demands are being made on sales and by whom at each stage. Take the time to make sure Marketing understands what value claims resonate with customers and what obstacles customers face internally when proposing to buy from you.

Reading analyst reports and talking to a few sales reps is not enough. Pull marketing staff away from content creation and send them into the reps' world. Have Marketers attend new sales training and sales meetings with customers. Let them listen in on telesales conversa-tions. Sales too must be willing to allow greater access to accounts, un-derstanding that a better-informed marketing organization that has stood in Sales' shoes will be a more valuable partner.

You can take another big step towards a Sales-Marketing partnership through a proactive, ongoing process for aligning objectives. Before committing to annual plans, hold direct conversations between Sales and Marketing about each organization's goals. Agree on how much of the sales pipeline marketing will be feeding, and what role it can and should play in accelerating the sales process once an opportunity is in the pipe. Jointly define the characteristics of a good lead, and the process for how leads from marketing activities will be pursued. Be sure that there is consensus on how to nurture and when to promote the "in-between" contacts that are promising but insufficiently "hot" for immediate sales action.

Periodically review how messaging, campaigns, and the sales process may be changing and why, and how best to communicate those changes to both organizations. Review what marketing tools and lead generation programs have, and have not, been useful in the field, and adjust future deliverables accordingly.

Educate Your Channels on What Matters

Sales is marketing's internal customer and, as with all customers, segmentation is a key to success here too.

If you're selling a complex product to large organizations, many people contribute to the sales process. Different sales process participants have different needs. Yet the focus of sales training is often on the content and tools more than on the audience. Sales is marketing's internal customer and, as with all customers, segmentation is a key to success here too. When you're thinking about the next sales kickoff or creating your sales enablement plan, ask yourself two key questions:

- Whom are you educating and enabling?

- What knowledge, tools, and skills does that person need to be successful?

One way to segment your sales resources is by current effectiveness. The top 20% of sales reps don't need, and won't accept, much education. They are likely to benefit from access to information and to a community of subject matter experts. The bottom 10% probably won't improve much regardless of training. The rest need information and skill-building on both the *what* of your products, and the *how* of sales processes and skills.

A person's role in the sales process is also key to designing education. Most companies with complex products already provide in-depth technical training to Sales Engineers. Consider similarly focused education for the rest of the sales team. Solution or product specialists need different information and skills than the global account managers, who must manage the customer relationship, and coordinate the rest of the account sales team.

First-line sales managers need coaching and interviewing skills they never used as individual reps. Regional directors may need to better understand lead generation techniques so they can provide informed input about programs in their region. In addition to phone skills, provide inside sales reps with information about the customer's business situation and the relevance of the current campaign. They are the first line of contact with those expensive leads. Their ability to actually engage in a conversation about the customer's business and needs, rather than just read the script, can drastically affect both the quantity and quality of opportunities entering your pipeline.

In designing their learning programs, Cisco strives to accommodate differences in the learning styles of the four generations that make up today's workforce: Traditionalists, born prior to 1945, Boomers, Gen Xers, and Millenials born after 1980. The youngest generation are DiSBies (digital since birth), and want interactive, even entertaining learning, a chance to explore, and a "connect me to everything" attitude. By contrast Gen Xers are more likely to respond to collaborative, team learning environments.[xiv] To serve all the audiences within your own organization, provide multiple modes for delivery of information and development of new skills.

There are other, less obvious, members of your sales team. Identify everyone who represents your company to customers, whether they have "sales" in their title or not. Who is staffing your booths at trade shows? Who is taking support calls? Who is answering online forum questions? Are there people at the executive briefing center who interact with customers? Do your professional services people know how to qualify a lead and what to communicate when they run across an opportunity? As part of your sales enablement efforts, inform all these people about how to position your company and products. And don't forget to make it easy for all of them to get leads or contacts into a tracking system that will ensure rapid follow-up.

Finally, don't forget about the other sales force that isn't on your payroll. They work for your partners, and even your customers. Add education and sales tools for channel partners to every sales enablement play you have. (See Rule 41 for more on empowering partners.) When you provide useful information to customers, include easy ways to pass that information on to their colleagues.

39 Features Don't Sell Products, Reps Do

Reps need to know how your customers think about their customers.

Great sales people don't sell. They collaborate with customers to design the best solution to their most pressing challenge. How can we get the rest of the sales force to do the same? Presentations about product features and competitive poison pills and silver bullets are a start. But they're not enough.

Customers surveyed about the sales process indicated that their top complaints were failure to listen, lack of understanding of customer needs, and inability to demonstrate value or craft a compelling solution.[xv] The skill development required to do these better is lacking from the bulk of product-heavy training curriculums. While product knowledge is important, it's entirely insufficient. Allocate some of the precious sales time to "soft skills" and domain expertise in customers' businesses.

Build domain expertise in the business processes, industries, and use cases where your products are relevant. Educate reps about what drives their prospects' business, how they solve their biggest issues, and what threats and opportunities they face. Reps need to know how your customers think about their customers, and what they consider their most critical business metrics. Without this knowledge, sales can focus only on your product, not on the customer's needs. Domain expertise gives reps the ability to place your products and services in the context of the customer's overall business objectives and the buyer's personal and role-based agenda.

Give sales the operational context for the product. Who will the actual users be? What other products will they use with yours? How often and in what kind of business and physical environment will they interact with your solution? Only by understanding these contextual factors can the rep actively collaborate with the customer on defining the best solution.

We assume anyone in sales already has great communication skills. Most are articulate, and fast on their feet. That's not enough. Polish communication skills by teaching reps to ask questions, and listen for true pain (the kind that justifies budget). Develop observation skills and the awareness to recognize the prospect's preferred communication mode, and to make adjustments to their own style to create rapport and trust with a variety of buyers. Raise awareness of how their own decision-making style influences their assumptions about how prospects make decisions.

Build up long-term account planning practices. Make sure reps understand the cross-sell and up-sell chain among your products and services, and know how to lay the groundwork for future deals even as they focus on this quarter's quota. Teach reps to identify and engage multiple decision makers within their accounts, and provide the tools and messages to engage each one. (Expanding the base of contacts accelerates deals, but also protects your customer relationship if a key contact leaves the company.)

"A man pretty much always refuses another man's first offer, no matter what it is," said Mark Twain. Don't assume sales reps are great negotiators. Their previous success may have come at the cost of too many margin-eroding compromises. Their negotiation approach may, or may not, reinforce your company's corporate culture and brand identity. The wrong kind of negotiation style may damage a relationship for years to come (long after the rep has moved on), or create unrealistic expectations. Hone their negotiation skills and be explicit about both *how* you prefer the rep to negotiate, and *what* is or is not negotiable in various types of deals.

Ultimately, sales education has to cover both the "what" and the "how" of successfully performing the individual's role within the sales cycle. Combining these skills, the rep can help the customer become an active participant in defining the solution, and create value within the sales process itself.

40 Put Training Wheels on Your Sales Initiatives

Big changes in multiple factors require lots of in-deal hand-holding.

Sales reps sell the products they know best, into opportunities they understand, to people they are familiar with, using tools they've succeeded with before. That's why sales adoption is one of the greatest challenges to any new go-to-market initiative. Even when done with sales input and lots of customer intelligence, introducing a new sales strategy is akin to learning to ride a bike. The amount of time before the training wheels come off will vary.

Expanding sales reps' comfort zone requires a broad array of training, support, and incentives. CA has seen the rewards of such a multi-faceted sales enablement approach. To implement a new use case based sales strategy, reps who had been selling product features to mid-level technical buyers would now be asked to speak to non-technical decision makers about the key metrics of mission-critical business processes. The marketing team provided comprehensive, hands-on sales enablement. They started with a global sales training tour. Senior executives actively promoted the new approach and initial sales successes. Though feedback on the tools and the training was overwhelmingly positive, most reps were still reluctant to put the new concepts to work in the field. The industry marketing staff stayed closely involved with every major deal in the pipeline. Still, widespread adoption took time, coaching, encouragement, and frequent repetition.

Do you need such a broad enablement effort for every new sales initiative? That depends on how many of the following are changing: features, pricing and packaging, products, competitors, partners, the problem you're solving, the scope of impact on your customers' business, the decision makers and influencers you need to engage.

The simplest change is the addition of new features to solve the same problem for the same buyer. In this case, Sales needs to know how the new capabilities will benefit the customer. A short information session and updates to product content are sufficient.

The introduction of new products that solve new problems is more complex, even when the buyers remain the same. These require learning the new product, pricing, and competitors, and grasping a new set of customer needs and benefits. For any cross-sell or up-sell opportunities, Sales must be able to connect the issues addressed by old and new products. Plan to educate on the same content multiple times: ahead of the product announcement, again in preparation for launch, and then again after the product attains initial market traction.

Create sales tools for each audience and stage in the sales process, and provide simple ways to find and use those tools. Demonstrate unwavering and consistent executive advocacy and on-site support for key deals by product managers or specialists. Even after you've done all that, be ready to nudge, encourage, and run behind the bike while Sales cautiously tests the new ideas. Consider monetary incentives to give the new product an extra push.

When new buyers are involved, the sales organization may need a whole new skillset. Reps comfortable speaking to IT managers may not have the confidence and expertise to engage business buyers or senior IT executives. Reps who are comfortable with a specific industry or business process may have to learn a whole new language. They may find that discussing $100,000 deals was easy, but that $1.5 million feels too big.

The most complex jump occurs when everything changes at once. With enough training and support, top sales people can sometimes make this complex shift. For the most part, however, big changes in multiple factors require the assistance of specialists and lots of in-deal hand-holding. Even so, training wheels may not be enough. When introducing drastically different sales requirements, plan on hiring at least some new sales resources.

41

Partners Are (Sales) People Too

Think of partners as both a customer segment and a sales force.

You've assigned portions of your target markets to indirect channels, clearly delineated territories, and created a compensation structure that adequately rewards channel partners. Ready to see the extra revenue come rolling in? Not quite. Just like sales reps, channel partners need adequate education and tools to sell effectively. Compare the support, training, and enablement you give to sales reps compares to what you provide to partners. If you are neglecting your partners, you are forfeiting a critical source of revenue growth.

Unfortunately, the battles over account coverage and compensation that typically accompany channel diversification create an attitude that the channel is "expensive." There is a reluctance to invest substantial additional resources in channel training and enablement. As a result, even companies with mature partner programs often leave this critical step to an afterthought. After all, the thinking goes, aren't we paying them enough to come up with their own campaigns and marketing materials?

Actually, no. Most resellers and systems integrators, especially the effective ones, have many vendors vying for their attention. Beyond compensation, making your products the easiest to sell and your company the easiest to work with gives you a critical competitive advantage.[xvi] Providing training and content to the channel also promotes consistency of message wherever your brand is sold.

To maximize channel revenue, think of partners as both a customer segment (or two or three) and a sales force. By thinking of partners as customers, you can focus in on their needs and interests. Understand what value you can provide above and beyond channel margin. Determine how your partners sell, and to whom. Find out how their sales people decide which partners to highlight, and how their marketing people decide to allocate marketing budget. Even after the partnership agreement is signed, these ongoing decisions are mini-sales—make sure your channel managers know how to influence them in your favor.

By thinking about partners as a sales force, you will include sales strategies, tools, and training for partners in your sales enablement plan. Add partner enablement as a key part of any new product introduction and go-to-market strategy. The organizations responsible for educating and arming internal sales should have partners within their scope, or work closely with the channel organization.

Help partners understand your products, and your value propositions. Though some partners may be savvier about a specific market or domain than your own reps, others will need more education. Teach them about the end-customers' needs and how your products help meet these. Recommend cross-vendor solutions that incorporate your products. Create "campaigns in a box" or other packaged go-to-market vehicles that your channel partners can customize easily.

To ensure its partner community can sell, Citrix holds an annual partner conference. The event, similar to a sales kickoff, provides partners with training and information about the latest products and market developments. The company defines how its products work together to address a particular need and assesses the overall market opportunity. Citrix shares this intelligence with partners during the conference, and throughout the year. Armed with this knowledge, partners are able to segment their accounts and determine the appropriate sales approach. Citrix also designs "go-to-market plays" every year. The company packages and provides these to partners, who then determine how best to leverage the campaigns with their own customers.

A word of caution: Do not leave partner enablement to individual channel reps. Without a systematic partner enablement program, channel managers are left to distribute collateral that your marketing group designed for direct sales use. If your objective is to ensure loyalty, effectiveness, and consistency of message among partners, you'll have to do better than that. Companies that focus on channel development as a core go-to-market requirement lay the groundwork for broad-based revenue growth and create nearly insurmountable barriers for competitors.

These Are Our Rules. What Are Yours?

According to Douglas Adams (The Hitchhiker's Guide to the Galaxy), 42 is the answer to Life, the Universe, and Everything. Maybe that's true for space travelers of the future. For B2B companies, however, 42 is just a modest start.

If you're breaking rules, making up new ones, or just implementing the established set, share them with fellow business executives. Visit http://www.RevenueOrchard.com and add your own rules to the 43 Rules (that's 42 plus yours) area.

A Resources

Great Resources

In researching this book, I discovered many interesting business resources that are useful insightful, or just plain intriguing and fun. Please share your favorites with me at lilia@shirmangroup.com.

Enterprise tools:

Socialtext - How much knowledge and expertise is hidden behind the titles and functional roles in your company? Socialtext provides the tools to foster interaction and overcome the restrictions that organizational structures place on collaboration. Credited with creating the "enterprise 2.0" concept, Socialtext has a growing list of tools to enable cross-functional collaboration.
http://www.socialtext.com

Crowdcast - This new company has taken the science of market prediction mechanisms and created a surprisingly simple—even fun—system for harnessing the hidden intelligence in organizations to create accurate and timely business planning insights. I was blown away by how much accuracy can be improved through collecting the wisdom of an employee base.
http://www.crowdcast.com

Xobni - Ok, so this isn't really an enterprise tool. Its more a personal sanity tool. If you or your employees are using Outlook, there might be a bit...ok, some...tons? of information buried deep in those emails. This helps find it—fast. Its inbox, spelled backwards.
http://www.xobni.com

Books:

- 'Blue Ocean Strategy' by W. Chan Kim and Renee Mauborgne
- 'Selling to Big Companies' by Jill Konrath
- 'Presentation Zen' by Garr Reynolds
- 'The Back of the Napkin' by Dan Roam
- 'How Great Decisions Get Made' by Don Maruska
- 'Inbound Marketing' by Brian Halligan, Dharmesh Shah, and David Meerman Scott

Associations and Research Sources:

- CSO Insights provides lots of detailed and insightful data on everything to do with the art and science of sales.
  http://www.csoinsights.com
- Marketing Profs All things marketing, from complex strategies to data on tactics to thought-provoking case studies.
  http://www.marketingprofs.com
- Association of Strategic Alliance Professionals provides resources and local networking opportunities to help you ensure this oft-neglected virtual part of your sales force is as productive as possible.
  http://www.strategic-alliances.org
- Gallup runs a seemingly endless array of surveys around the world to gauge opinions and attitudes on every imaginable topic.
  http://www.gallup.com

B Bibliography

i. Kim Chan W., and Renee Mauborgne. *Blue Ocean Strategy.* Harvard Business School Press 2006.

ii. Porter, M.E. *Competitive Strategy.* New York: Free Press, 1980.

iii. Aiken, Carolyn B., and Scott P. Keller. *The CEO's role in leading transformation.* Mindspring Blog, Feb 2007 (http://tinyurl.com/yf8ey5s).

iv. Mindspring Blog. "1982 University of Wisconsin study" As described in *The CEO's role in leading transformation.* Feb 2007.

v. Buckingham, Marcus, and Donald Clifton. *Now, Discover Your Strengths.* The Free Press, 2001.

vi. Stephen Hawking with Leonard Mlodinow. *A Briefer History of Time.* Bantam, 2005.

vii. Markides, Constantinos C. "To Diversify or Not to Diversify." In *Harvard Business Review on Strategies for Growth.* Harvard Business School Press, 1998.

viii. Wikipedia, *Market* http://en.wikipedia.org/wiki/Market.

ix. Adhikari, Richard. *Social Networks Among Trends in CRM for 2009.* InternetNews.com, Dec 2008.
Mirrissey, Brian. *Forrester: Social Web Now Mainstream.* AdWeek, Oct 2008.

x. *Industry Specialization by B2B Vendors Benchmark Study.* The Shirman Group, 2009.

xi. *Industry Specialization in Enterprise Software Benchmarking Study.* The Shirman Group, 2008.

xii. *2009 Sales Effectiveness Survey.* CSO Insights, 2009.

xiii. *Second Annual CMO Survey.* Red Herring, February 2007.

xiv. Stein, Dave. *Technology-Driven Sales Learning at Cisco.* Dave Stein's Blog. http://tinyurl.com/yzvjwvg.

xv. Wellesley Hills Group. *How Clients Buy: 2009 Benchmark Report.* Rain Today study, 2009.

xvi. Stuart, Bruce. *The Channels Handbook.* Channel Corp, 2000.

About the Author

Lilia Shirman is a technology industry executive, author, and advisor. She is the founder and Managing Director of The Shirman Group, a consulting firm that helps technology innovators identify and pursue new revenue streams and growth opportunities. Shirman Group clients include large companies like BEA Systems/Oracle, CA, Intervoice, and Symantec, as well as rapidly growing new ventures. Before founding The Shirman Group, Lilia held leadership roles in product, solution, and industry marketing, strategic alliances, and business development at BEA Systems. She also helped firms including HP, Cisco, and Compaq with corporate operations and planning as part of Accenture's strategy practice.

Lilia also serves on the Advisory Boards and as an interim executive of early stage ventures, and is a coach in Stanford University's Global Entrepreneurial Marketing program. She holds a B.S. in Engineering from U.C. Berkeley, and an M.S. in Technology Management from Stanford University.

42 Rules Program

A lot of people would like to write a book, but only a few actually do. Finding a publisher, and distributing and marketing the book are challenges that prevent even the most ambitious authors from getting started.

If you want to be a successful author, we'll provide you the tools to help make it happen. Start today by completing a book proposal at our website http://superstarpress.com/.

For more information, email info@superstarpress.com or call 408-257-3000.

Other Happy About Books

42 Rules™ of Marketing

Compilation of ideas, theories, and practical approaches to marketing challenges that marketers know they should do, but don't always have the time or patience to do.

Paperback:$19.95
eBook:$11.45

42 Rules™ for Successful Collaboration

Whether you are a 5-person team or a 50,000 person company some of the same rules for successful collaboration apply. The more you share what you know the more it is worth; understanding a person's local context is more critical to successful collaboration than any technology you may use.

Paperback:$19.95
eBook:$14.95

42 Rules™ of Employee Engagement

Susan Stamm will inspire and challenge you to create a unique workspace with your team that attracts and inspires high performance, commitment and authentic work relationships. This book is loaded with practical advice and actions you can take away to begin building an engaged team.

Paperback:$19.95
eBook:$14.95

42 Rules™ for Creating WE

'42 Rules for Creating WE' offers new insights from thought leaders in neuroscience, organizational development, and brand strategy, introducing groundbreaking practices for bringing the spirit of WE to any organization, team or cause.

Paperback:$19.95
eBook:$14.95

Purchase these books at Happy About
http://happyabout.info/
or at other online and physical bookstores.

A Message From Super Star Press™

Thank you for your purchase of this 42 Rules Series book. It is available online at:
http://42rules.com/growing_enterprise_revenue/ or at other online and physical bookstores. To learn more about contributing to books in the 42 Rules series, check out http://superstarpress.com.

Please contact us for quantity discounts at
sales@superstarpress.com.

If you want to be informed by email of upcoming books, please email
bookupdate@superstarpress.com.

CPSIA information can be obtained at www.ICGtesting.com
Printed in the USA
LVOW12s2334140514

385875LV00015B/221/P